# 7
## MISTAKES EVERY
## INVESTOR MAKES...
## AND HOW TO AVOID THEM

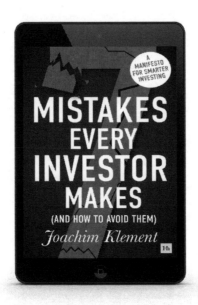

# 7

# MISTAKES EVERY INVESTOR MAKES…

## AND HOW TO AVOID THEM

### A MANIFESTO FOR SMARTER INVESTING

## JOACHIM KLEMENT

Hh

HARRIMAN HOUSE LTD
3 Viceroy Court
Bedford Road
Petersfield
Hampshire
GU32 3LJ
GREAT BRITAIN
Tel: +44 (0)1730 233870
Email: enquiries@harriman-house.com
Website: www.harriman-house.com

First published in Great Britain in 2020

Paperback ISBN: 978-0-85719-770-2
eBook ISBN: 978-0-85719-771-9

British Library Cataloguing in Publication Data
A CIP catalogue record for this book can be obtained from the British Library.

# CONTENTS

# ABOUT THE AUTHOR

Joachim Klement is a research analyst and former chief investment officer with 20 years' experience in financial markets. He spent most of his career working with wealthy individuals and family offices advising them on investments and helping them manage their portfolios. He also managed equity portfolios for banks and independent asset managers. Most recently, Joachim worked as head of investment research for a small investment bank in the City of London, helping pension funds, insurance companies and other institutional investors understand the chaos of today's market and make better investment decisions. Throughout his career, Joachim has worked with individual investors and institutions from the US to Europe and Asia.

Joachim studied mathematics and physics at the Swiss Federal Institute of Technology (ETH) in Zurich, Switzerland and graduated with a master's degree in mathematics. During his time at ETH, Joachim experienced the technology bubble of the late 1990s first hand. Through this work, he became interested in finance and investments and studied business administration at the Universities of Zurich and Hagen, Germany, graduating with a master's degree in economics and finance and switching into the financial services industry in time for the run-up to the financial crisis. His friends tell him never to switch industries again, since a few years after, the entire industry tends to collapse.

# ACKNOWLEDGEMENTS

Writing this book has felt like a pregnancy. I have been carrying more and more weight around with me and then, in one quick but painful rush, it popped out. But, as with every pregnancy, one cannot do it alone. I would like to thank first and foremost my editor, Craig Pearce, along with the entire team at Harriman House, all of whom have helped this project come to fruition – in a sense, they were the midwife that supported me through the process of giving birth. And like all midwives around the world, they deserve lots of praise for what they do. Thank you also to the great team at the Naval and Military Club in London, where most of this book was written. It was a great place to go to work and focus on the tasks at hand.

But as I said, this book did not come out of nothing and is the product of years of research and conversation with many people. I would especially like to thank two mentors of mine, Prof. Klaus Wellershoff and the late Andreas Höfert, who have taught me more about economics, investments and the art of critical thinking than anybody else. I owe them a lot of gratitude for the many discussions and support they have given me over the years. Furthermore, I want to thank the sons of Klaus Wellershoff, whose "reality hits you hard, bro" had to make it into this book. It was just too good to be missed.

Over the past two years, I have spoken to many people who have encouraged me to write this book and helped me refine its contents. It all started with a series of short papers that I wrote for Fidante Partners which, after being deemed too 'risky' for the business, were never published. As I told my wonderful boss, Cathy Hales, and my colleague, Gihan Ismail, at the time, even though it won't be published with a Fidante brand, it might still lead to something else. Thank you both for giving me the leeway to spin my crazy ideas and letting me push the envelope. And thank you for all the support and encouragement you have given me, no matter where my crazy ideas led.

There is also a whole list of people who provided discussion, invaluable feedback on draft versions of this book or input to the original papers on which it is based:

Brett Arends, Dewi John, Tim Koroknay, Sam Morris, Larry Siegel, Paolo Sironi, Jason Voss and Jason Zweig. Thank you all very much.

Finally, and most importantly, I want to thank my wife, Robin Miranda, who is my most enthusiastic supporter, my fiercest critic and always asks the right questions. Without her, none of this could have happened. This book is dedicated to her.

# INTRODUCTION, OR HOW A RELAY OF MISERY CAN LEAD TO GOOD THINGS

I always wanted to write a self-help book. You know the kind of book: if you follow these three steps, you will get rich, smart, beautiful, etc. When it comes to investing, these books have titles like *The Instant Millionaire* or *I Invested in Amazon at the IPO: Here is how you can find the next Amazon*. My friends and I call them 'investment porn'. Most of the time, the only people with any chance of becoming an instant millionaire with these books are the authors.

My problem is that I am plagued by this thing people call 'conscience' or 'integrity'. I know, it's such a 20th century thing. We live in the 21st century, when the ability to ignore pesky little things like facts and data has seemingly become a necessary condition of a political or business leader. If you want to gain a large following these days, it seems your promises have to be big and your delusions even bigger. But I have news for you: you can only ignore facts and data for so long before eventually "reality hits you hard, bro," as the kids of a friend of mine used to say.

My career as an investor started in the late 1990s during the technology bubble, when investors were convinced that the internet would revolutionise the world. Every business that was involved in the new economy attracted more money than it could spend and saw its valuations go through the roof.

I was in the middle of this hype myself. On the one hand, I invested in technology stocks in the late 1990s and lost a large amount of money when the bubble burst in the early 2000s. But, on the other hand, I was working in this new economy. I was helping to run a small spin-off company at my university that helped people find jobs via the internet.

I know this sounds quaint today, but back in the mid-1990s setting up a job site on the internet was revolutionary. And business was going well. We made so much money with our little internet company that we couldn't spend it fast enough. And since we were all volunteers and had regular day jobs, we didn't have the time to grow the company aggressively. But with the success of this company came the delusion that starting and running a business was easy.

How wrong we were. In early 2000, the company's revenue dried up almost instantaneously and our sense of self-importance crashed together with the business. Our saving grace was that we had other jobs and had not burnt through the money the business made in the good times. These savings helped the business survive for the next three years, when it finally stopped losing money.

Today, the company still exists but, just like a quarter century ago, it is a small business run by graduates of my alma mater as a hobby. Nobody ever got rich from it but, over the years, countless graduates had the chance to learn what it takes to run a business on a day-to-day basis. And the business allowed them to make mistakes on a small scale without endangering their livelihoods.

The mistakes I made during the technology bubble, both in running a business and as an investor, stayed with me for the rest of my life. They inform my decisions to this day and will likely continue to do so.

But while these mistakes were amongst the first I made, they were by no means the last. Instead, they just set me off on what I like to call my personal relay of misery. Sometimes, I look back at my career as an investor and it seems like I just went from one mistake to the next. The fact is, investing is not simple. No matter what self-help books try to tell us, there is no simple or quick way to success. Mistakes are inevitable.

Whether they admit it or not, every investor in the world has made lots of mistakes in their career and will continue to do so. I am no exception and you, dear reader, aren't either. Even Warren Buffett makes mistakes, time and again. But what differentiates the good investors from the poor ones (and the authors of self-help books, I might add) is their willingness to admit these mistakes, accept the consequences of their decisions and learn from them.

This process of learning is what makes investors better over time. In this sense, each investor's relay of misery can teach us how to become better at investing ourselves.

# Let me take you on my journey

This book is my effort to help investors become better. I won't do it by promising you a quick way to investment success. Instead, I can only offer you a look at the blood, sweat and tears I have spilled over the years to get better myself. My hope is that as you read about the mistakes I have made, you will be able to avoid them yourself and learn faster than I did.

The problem with this endeavour is that I have made so many mistakes that they could fill a small library. However, in my experience, there are some that are more common than others. Equally, some actions are often not even recognised as errors in the broader investment community, but instead considered good practice.

In this book, I focus on the mistakes I made as an investor that I think are very common. I see other investors, both private and professional, make them today. In fact, while this book is written in an accessible style that is geared towards private investors, professional investors will likely benefit from it as well. While they may be aware of the pitfalls explained in some chapters, they might not be aware of others and may still make these mistakes today.

In every chapter, I not only review the mistakes, but show why a particular investment habit can lead to poor performance. Remember, this is an honest self-help book and thus, I want to help you help yourself. Most importantly, I also present the scientific evidence for why these mistakes are bad for performance. At the end of each chapter, I explain the tools and techniques that I have developed over the years, and that I use in my investments, to avoid these mistakes and create better performance.

The downside of this approach is that, sometimes, this book will dive somewhat deeper into the technicalities of investing. But, rest assured, it will all be explained in terms that every investor who is interested in the topic and has managed their own portfolio will understand.

# My selection of the seven most common mistakes

The next seven chapters provide an overview of the seven most common mistakes that investors make. And, as I have said, I am guilty of committing all of them at some point in the past.

**Chapter 1** focuses on an area that many professional and private investors often won't even consider a mistake: forecasting. Investing is about identifying the best assets to own going forward. As we all know, past performance is a poor and unreliable guide to future outcomes. What good is an investment if it had great performance for the past five years but tanks after you buy it?

As I mentioned, I started my career at the height of the tech bubble, when technology stocks had performed well for the previous five to ten years but, for the next decade, performed poorly. So, obviously, successful investing requires a certain degree of forecasting. If you can make better forecasts of the risks and returns of a specific investment than other investors, you can achieve a better performance than they do.

But the forecasts of even the best experts in the world can sometimes go horribly wrong. The most prominent failure in recent history was the global financial crisis of 2008. So many experts failed to see that crisis coming that the Queen of England, when opening a new building for the London School of Economics in November 2008, asked the room full of world-leading experts: "Why did nobody notice it?"

It isn't just high-profile forecasting failures like this that can hurt our performance as investors. Analysts and economists make forecasts all the time but, as I will show, these forecasts are usually not worth the paper they are printed on. If you think that experts are bad at forecasting, you haven't even seen half of it.

In Chapter 1, I show you that expert forecasts are so unreliable that it is better for investors to ignore them altogether. But if we shouldn't rely on the forecasts of experts, and we can't rely on past performance, how are we supposed to invest? At the end of the chapter, I show you that not all forecasts are useless, but that we have to be very humble and include the uncertainty around these forecasts in our investment decisions. The answer that emerges is remarkably simple, but effective.

**Chapter 2** looks at our tendency to fixate on the short term. It has become a common complaint that the world is becoming too short-term oriented. Companies manage their results on a quarterly basis, and investors want to see positive returns on their investment every year, abandoning investments after a temporary setback.

Yet, as I discuss, so many of our daily habits as investors encourage short-term thinking. The constant news flow about the latest developments in the markets blurs our vision for long-term developments and entices us to react to short-term fluctuations. And the incentives of professional money managers, as well as business leaders, tend to be short-term in nature.

Even after the financial crisis, when incentive structures were changed and focused more on the long term, the best we can hope for is a three-year outlook. Even that is too short, as I will show. If we want to be successful in the long run, we need to evaluate our investments from a true long-term perspective. And we need to work with people who have a similar long-term outlook. Only then are the incentives of everyone aligned properly, something that greatly enhances our chances of being successful.

But wait. There is another mistake investors make. In their efforts to avoid short-termism, investors can become too long-term oriented. If that sounds counter-intuitive, then you need to read **Chapter 3**. After all, every investment book, and financial planner, that is worth something will tell you that the key to success is a long-term orientation.

Avoid the temptation of short-term market swings and you are going to be fine. I agree with the first part of this sentence. The problem is that by avoiding short-term fluctuations, we sometimes become trapped in an untenable long-term position that has no chance of ever becoming profitable. This is when a long-term orientation has gone wrong and becomes an investment mistake.

In my view, the key to investment success is to find the right balance between short- and long-termism. In Chapter 3, I focus on two techniques that have helped me tremendously, over the last decade or so, to find this balance.

Then I move on to a topic that has fascinated me for the better part of two decades now, but is rarely discussed in the investment community: the role our experiences play in investment success or failure. **Chapter 4** demonstrates something that probably won't be much of a surprise to many readers, namely, that markets tend to repeat past mistakes over and over again. But it's not just markets that repeat mistakes, it's investors as well – investors are terrible at learning from their own mistakes. This, as I show, can give rise to market bubbles and crashes.

What good is it to know about these mistakes if we don't learn from them? Improving your performance requires learning from past experience, which is only possible if we systematically review past investments and draw the right conclusions. Chapter 4 will provide you with some crucial tools that allow you to learn from past experience and systematically improve your performance over time.

As you read through the common mistakes outlined in this book, one of the reactions I expect you to have is: "Yes, that is a stupid mistake to make, but I would never do that." You might even think that right now, as you read through the summary of what lies ahead.

People, when pressed, generally tend to make excuses for how their mistakes were unpredictable or not really mistakes at all. Nobody likes to admit mistakes and that is a common mistake in itself. It is a form of confirmation bias, the human tendency to discount information that contradicts our previously held beliefs and emphasise information that confirms them. This confirmation bias is also active in our investment decisions. We love to be right about our investments so, when things go wrong, we tend to find all kinds of excuses for why they did go wrong.

Unfortunately, the excuses often aren't honest. A common problem is partially examining an investment, emphasising why the investment should be a great one and downplaying or ignoring the risk. But you can ignore the risks only for so long. Often, risks that could have been foreseen – but were readily ignored – materialise and create a lot of damage in our portfolios. **Chapter 5** focuses on these processes and techniques to mitigate these mistakes.

**Chapter 6** shifts away from investments you make yourself towards the topic of delegating investments to professional money managers. Nobody is an expert in everything, and it is wise to delegate some investment decisions to professionals and experts. However, when we select mutual funds and other investments that are managed by professionals, we often make mistakes. One of the most common mistakes in this domain is, again, to focus too much on past performance and short-term developments. But there are other mistakes as well.

As I will show, money managers are in a constant race to attract as much investor money as they possibly can. One way to do this is to achieve great performance. But there are other forces at play and they can lead investors astray. The end result is that too much money is invested in funds and money managers that have no realistic chance of achieving success. The long-term result is then, too often, a significantly lower performance than the overall market.

In Chapter 6, I focus on some basic tools that can be used by every investor to reduce the likelihood of failure when delegating investments to professionals.

If all of that isn't enough to make you a better investor, I have one last tip for you in **Chapter 7**. In my opinion, the current mainstream view of how financial markets work is incomplete at best, and completely off the mark at worst.

As I will explain, there are three basic assumptions about how markets work that are ingrained in our current understanding of them. But what if these fundamental assumptions are wrong? What if our entire understanding of markets is built on sand?

In Chapter 7, I introduce you to some intriguing ideas of where traditional finance theory might be wrong, and what that means for financial markets and investors. If you allow me, I will take you down a rabbit hole into the fascinating world of complex dynamic systems – an adventure that will rival Alice's own in Wonderland. And just as Alice emerged from Wonderland a bit wiser, so too will you emerge from this chapter a bit wiser and with a new perspective on what is and isn't possible in markets.

But be aware that Chapter 7 introduces a perspective on markets that is still evolving and part of ongoing research. All is in flux as, indeed, is your own journey as an investor.

As I will show you in the concluding **Chapter 8**, this book cannot be the solution to all your problems. If it were, it would probably sell many more copies. Instead, this book is the beginning. I do not have the secret sauce for investment success, the strategy that will make you rich, or the investment tip to end all your money woes. Nobody has. All I can do, in this book, is set you off on your own journey to become a better investor.

I can be your guide for the first few steps but, ultimately, you will have to venture out on your own. What I hope to do is equip you with the right tools to be successful in that venture.

,

# CHAPTER 1

## THE SHORTEST INVESTMENT JOKE: MY FORECAST HAS A DECIMAL POINT

On 7 December 2018, the *Financial Times* reported, under the headline "Market predictions: 2019 to bring new level of uncertainty", that investment strategists expected market uncertainty to prevail in 2019. Furthermore, the *FT* reported that the "median forecast of strategists" indicated that the US economy would grow by 2.6% in real terms and the S&P 500 would end the year at 3,090 points.

At the time the article was published, the S&P 500 stood at 2,633 points, so the average expectation of strategists was for a 17.5% rally in little more than a year. Most strategists expected the S&P 500 to rise in 2019, but the most pessimistic forecast called for a 9% decline.

It has become somewhat of a rite of passage for strategists to be interviewed by newspapers at the end of each year about their expectations for the next 12 months. The requests for forecasts come in by the dozen from newspapers, TV stations and magazines alike. Some outlets even run horse races comparing the accuracy of forecasts at the end of the year to crown the best forecaster, who will then forever be known as the person who predicted the current bull/bear market or the last recession/recovery (choose your adjectives depending on the actual market behaviour). In extreme cases, economists or strategists who call for a financial crisis or a severe bear market in advance can become global superstars.

The temptation is high for economists and strategists not to provide forecasts that are qualitative in nature, but to instead make precise forecasts for the return of the stock market or the growth of the economy with several digits after the decimal point. This reminds me of a quip by novelist William Gilmore Simms, that "economists put decimal points into their forecasts to show they have a sense of humour".

The excerpts from the newspaper article above already demonstrates why this approach is problematic. The most pessimistic forecast called for a significant decline in the stock market from the already depressed levels at the time (remember that the S&P 500 dropped more than 10% in the fourth quarter of 2018), while the median forecast called for a massive rally. The fact that the median was 17.5% means that half of the surveyed strategists called for stock market returns in excess of that. Thus, according to a bunch of experts on financial markets, the return of the S&P 500 in 2019 could be anything from –10% to more than 20%.

*What use is a single forecast from this collection, if the uncertainty around it is so large?*

Some would argue that these return forecasts are marketing exercises that no investor would ever take seriously. Yet I know of several strategists and economists who produce such forecasts on a regular basis in their jobs, even though they know they are not worth the paper they are printed on. Instead, they say that their clients, be they professional or retail investors, want these numbers so they can decide how to allocate their portfolios.

I have been in several meetings where clients have greeted me with the question: "What's your number?" In one job I had, after I provided an outlook for the new year, the first question asked was about the consensus forecasts for the stock market. Investors take these forecasts not just seriously, but literally.

Nevertheless, I don't think strategists make these precise forecasts simply to please their clients or journalists. After all, they keep making extremely precise forecasts even in circumstances when hardly anyone is looking. Here is an excerpt from a research report on Geely Automotive, the Chinese car manufacturer and owner of Volvo and other brands:

> "In view of the slightly lower sales volume expectation due to market weakness, more than offset by better-than-expected price resilience, we raise our fiscal year 2019–2020 revenue forecast by 2.5–3.6%. However, with more prudent margin assumptions, given increasing costs, such as emission standard upgrade and research and development, we only increase our earnings forecast by 0.8%."

The analyst then goes on to predict that Geely would sell 1,618,939 cars in 2019, 1,753,079 cars in 2020 and 1,858,030 cars in 2021. Profit margins are expected to be 19.7% in 2019 and 19.9% in 2020, before falling back to 19.7% in 2021. And these forecasts are presented alongside 15 pages of extremely detailed tables modelling every aspect of the company's balance sheet, cash flow statements and income statements. All this is used to recommend the share as an attractive investment opportunity for investors.

I am not sure if the recommendation would change if Geely sold 1,618,940 or even 1,618,938 cars in 2019, or if a profit margin of 19.8% instead of 19.7%, would make a difference to the analysis. But if it didn't make a difference, then I would argue that this analyst is using excessive precision which is irrelevant for the investment decision. Just because Excel can show seven digits of a number, does not mean you need to.

This chapter will focus on the impact this tendency towards forecasting developments that are essentially unknowable, or that have such high uncertainty around them that a point forecast is not reasonable, can have on investor portfolios. While precise forecasts can create a sense of certainty about the future, such certainty is entirely misplaced. First, I will show that forecasts like those above are highly unreliable and can create massive losses in a portfolio if they are only a little bit off the mark. Second, investment portfolios can be made more robust in changing market environments if the uncertainty of financial markets is taken seriously and incorporated into the portfolios of investors. How this can be done in practice will be the focus of the second part of this chapter.

## The future is uncertain – deal with it

I would not have a problem with precise forecasts if they were in any way reliable. However, as Figure 1.1 shows, the forecasts of strategists have been far off the mark in the past.

The figure shows the difference between the return of the S&P 500 as predicted by strategists at the beginning of each year and the actual return of the index in that year. For example, at the beginning of 1999, strategists predicted the S&P 500 to rise by 8.8%. It then rallied 19.5%, so the analysts were too pessimistic about the market by 10.8% (leftmost bar in Figure 1.1). In 2018, on the other hand, strategists expected the S&P 500 to rally 10.3% at the beginning of the year, but it declined by 6.2%. This meant that their forecasts were too optimistic by 16.6% (rightmost bar in Figure 1.1).

**Figure 1.1: Forecast error of analysts**

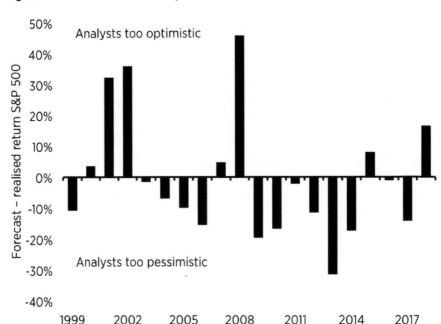

Source: Bloomberg.

In 13 of the last 20 years, strategists have been off the mark by more than 10%, while the median error of forecasts has been 4.6%. Compare this to the average annual return of 3.6% of the S&P 500 during the last 20 years and it becomes clear that these forecasts have an uncertainty associated with them that is roughly of the same order of magnitude as recent market returns.

Maybe I am being too hard on these poor strategists. Maybe we should pay less attention to the actual number and more to the direction they predict. Will the stock market go up or down next year? As it turns out, they got the direction of the stock market right in only nine out of the last 20 years (Figure 1.2). In other words, the ability of strategists to forecast the direction of the stock market is no better than the toss of a coin.

**Figure 1.2: How often do analysts get the direction of the stock market right?**

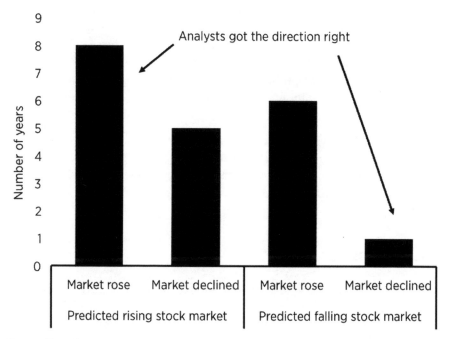

Source: Bloomberg.

These results are no accident. Professor Markus Spiwoks of the University of Applied Sciences in Wolfsburg, Germany, has investigated the forecasting ability of economists and strategists for years. As a former research analyst and portfolio manager, he and his colleague Oliver Hein looked at the forecasts of more than 400 experts surveyed by the ZEW (*Zentrum für Europäische Wirtschaftsforschung*) in Germany each month between 1995 and 2004. The experts tried to predict the return of six different stock markets in the US, Europe and Asia, as well as the ten-year government bond yields of six countries and the exchange rate movements between them. All the forecasts were made for a one-year period ahead.

The study results were unequivocal. In each case, the prediction error of the analysts was higher than the error of a naïve prediction that the market would be exactly the same in one year's time. Therefore, simply assuming that markets don't change at all delivered more reliable results than the combined expertise of 400 analysts and economists.

In a follow-up study of more than 150,000 forecasts of interest rates and bond yields in 12 countries, between 1989 and 2009, researchers found the same result. They also found that the correlation between forecasts and true interest rates was lower than the correlation between forecast rates and rates at the time when the forecasts were made. In almost every case, the forecasts better represented the situation at the time when the forecasts were made, then the actual events they tried to predict. When interest rates rose, analysts predicted they would continue to rise, and when interest rates declined, analysts predicted they would continue to decline. Turning points were rarely predicted and never with any degree of accuracy that would be helpful for investors. Extrapolating the current level of interest rates into the future should have done better than any of the individual analyst forecasts.

It seems that while analyst forecasts are guided by the present, they are not exactly the present. Analysts try to second-guess current interest rates and derive forecasts that are different from current rates. Unfortunately, this second-guessing leads to worse forecasts than just using the current interest rate.

## It gets worse...

Long-term investors may argue that the one-year forecasts I have discussed so far are not relevant to them, since they hold on to their investments for much longer time periods. And over the long run, these forecast errors could simply cancel each other out, so that, on average, the long-term investor would be just fine using these forecasts. As I have mentioned above, the average forecast error of strategists for the S&P 500 over the last 20 years has been 4.6% per year, so you probably should not get too optimistic.

A systematic analysis of the forecast error of different equity valuation approaches, by Amit Goyal and Ivo Welch, has indeed shown that uncertainty does not get smaller as the investment horizon increases. Testing several dozen methods to forecast the equity risk premium, i.e. the excess return of equities over long-term government bonds, they found that the forecast error *increases* as the forecast horizon increases.

Figure 1.3 shows the key result from their study, but it needs some explanation. First, while the researchers tested many different models for forecasting the equity risk premium, their most comprehensive model – aptly called 'the kitchen sink model' – put all the different approaches together. The hope was that the errors of different forecasting approaches would cancel each other out, and that the kitchen sink model would have a lower forecast error than the individual models. In fact, the kitchen sink model *did* perform a little bit better than most models, but not by much.

**Figure 1.3: Forecasting errors for the equity risk premium**

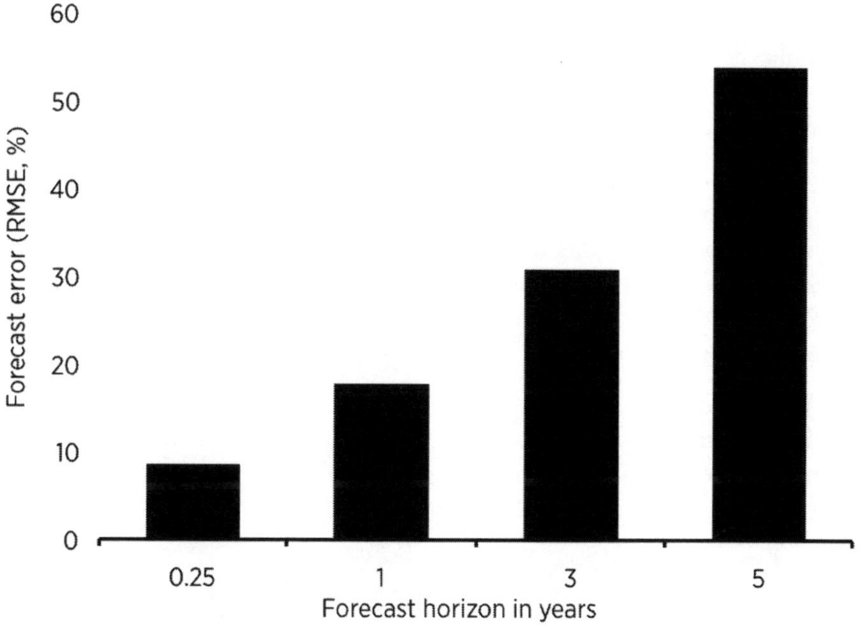

Source: Goyal and Welch (2008).

In any case, our chart shows the root mean squared error (RMSE) of the forecast relative to the true equity risk premium. The RMSE is a kind of average forecast error like the one I used in the example of forecasts for the S&P 500 above. It is calculated by first sorting all the forecasts made by the model each year for a given time horizon (e.g. one quarter or one year). For all the forecasts with the same time horizon, the average deviation of the forecasts from the true value is calculated. This RMSE is then divided by the average equity risk premium to calculate the relative forecast error.

For example, if the forecast horizon is one year and the relative deviation of the forecasts made in the past is 20% (in their study, Goyal and Welch use averages from 1902 to 2005), then this is the RMSE. If the true equity risk premium over the time frame was 5%, then the error in the forecast would be 20% x 5% = 1%. A model with a 20% relative error would thus come within ±1% of the true premium. Of course, these forecast errors are not the same each year, instead, they vary. The RMSE is designed in such a way that the error is expected to be within ±1% in two out of three cases. This means that if the forecast horizon is one year and the RMSE is 20%, the forecast error would be ±1%, and in two out of three years we should see the actual forecast lie within that range. In the third year, however, the error is expected to be larger than ±1%.

As Figure 1.3 shows, the sad truth is that forecast errors grow rapidly as the forecast horizon grows. A short-term oriented investor with an investment horizon of one quarter (0.25 years) faces a relative forecast error of 8.6%, which means that if the true equity risk premium is 5% (or 1.25% per quarter), the forecast is going to be between 1.15% and 1.35% in two out of three cases. That is pretty accurate and certainly nothing to worry about.

However, a long-term investor with a time horizon of five years faces much worse odds of being right. Thanks to the compound interest effect, a 5% equity risk premium per year grows to an outperformance of equities versus bonds of 27.6% after five years. But the relative forecast error grows to a whopping 53.9% as well, so that the forecast will typically be between 12.7% and 42.5%. That is an estimation error large enough to drive a train through.

In essence, all we can say over a five-year horizon is that equities significantly outperform bonds. However, it is pretty much anyone's guess if this is a small outperformance of 10% or so, or a massive outperformance of 40% or more.

## The uncertainty introduced by compound interest

These forecast errors are not the only form of uncertainty investors have to face. They just add to the fundamental uncertainty around future returns and their impact on the development of savings and investments.

The common wisdom is that investors should hold stocks and other risky assets for the long term because the uncertainty of the outcome is reduced as the investment horizon increases. There is clearly a lot of truth in this wisdom. For example, the probability that stocks will outperform bonds over the long term is higher than over the short term. Also, the probability that your equity portfolio will have a negative return declines as the investment horizon increases. Professor Jeremy Siegel of the University of Pennsylvania is one of the leading advocates of this argument and his book, *Stocks for the Long Run,* argues that as the investment horizon increases, stocks tend to have the highest returns and the likelihood of negative returns or underperformance, relative to other asset classes, shrinks.

Figure 1.4 shows a variation of the typical chart used to demonstrate this effect. Going back to 1983, I plotted the range of returns of the FTSE 100 stock market index in the UK for investment horizons ranging from one year to 15 years. In any given year, between 1983 and 2018, the return of the FTSE 100 was between −31% and +35%, with an average annual return of 6.7%. About one in three years showed a negative return. If you had invested in the FTSE 100 for 15 years without buying or selling any shares in between, then the best return you could have achieved was 12.5% per year (the years 1983 to 1998, during which the FTSE 100 grew almost six-fold). The worst return that an investor could achieve was −0.4% per year from 1999 to 2014. Thus, the range of returns, or the uncertainty around the average annual return, decreased significantly as the investment horizon increased. Annual average returns for the FTSE 100 seem less uncertain for long-term investors than for short-term investors.

Most importantly, the decline in the uncertainty of the range of returns as the investment horizon increases, also leads to a reduced likelihood of experiencing negative returns. The chances of experiencing a negative return with a 15-year investment horizon were about one-in-ten. If an investor had held on to the FTSE for 20 years, there wouldn't have been a single instance since 1983 when they would have experienced a negative return. Using data for the US that spans a much longer historical time period, Jeremy Siegel shows that the chances of losing money with stock market investments decline continuously as the investment horizon increases. It is easy to show that this is true for practically all stock markets in the world, with the exception of markets that have been disrupted by extreme events, like world wars, hyperinflation, or the nationalisation of entire swathes of the economy.

**Figure 1.4: Return distribution of the FTSE 100**

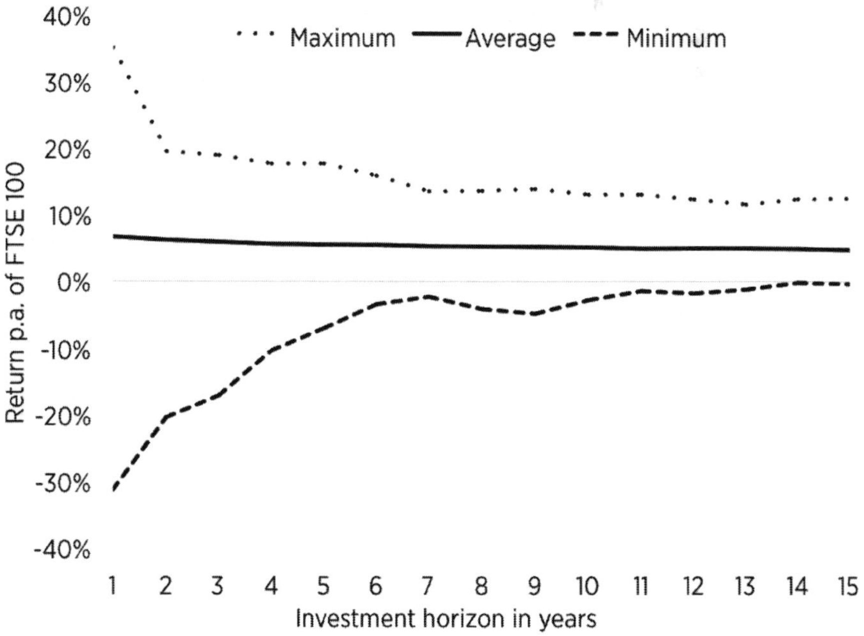

Source: Author's calculations.

Note that Figure 1.4 is not subject to any estimation errors because it looks at past performance that has been realised in the markets. I argue, however, that this reduction in uncertainty around average annual returns is a mirage. In fact, I argue that the uncertainty for the investor *increases* as the investment horizon increases.

## Increasing uncertainty

In order to see this, I have plotted what really matters to the investor in Figure 1.5 – the development of £1 invested in the FTSE 100. Note that this figure uses exactly the same data as Figure 1.4; it just changes the perspective from average returns to the wealth created by the investment. For all practical purposes, the value of an investment portfolio is more important to the investor than the average return earned over time.

As can be seen in Figure 1.5, the range of outcomes between the best and worst case does not narrow as it did in Figure 1.4. After one year, £1 invested in the FTSE 100 turned on average into £1.07, but the range of outcomes was anywhere between 69p and £1.35. If you had invested £1 in the FTSE 100 and then waited 15 years, the worst possible outcome was that this £1 turned into 95p and the best possible outcome was it turning into £5.88. That is a significant increase in the uncertainty around final wealth as the investment horizon increases. An investor saving for retirement for 15 years or longer faces a range of outcomes from losing a little bit of money in nominal terms (and a lot more when adjusted for inflation) to becoming extremely comfortable in retirement due to a large nest egg.

**Figure 1.5: Distribution of £1 invested in the FTSE 100**

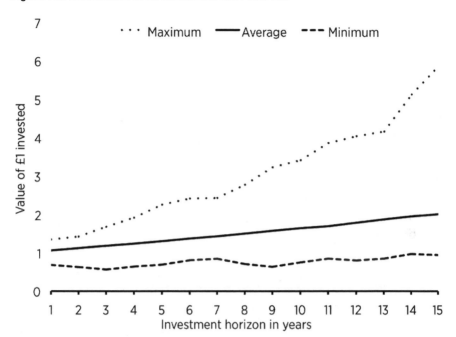

Source: Author's calculations.

The reason for this seeming contradiction between Figures 1.4 and 1.5 is that the range of outcomes in terms of returns narrows less over time than the range of portfolio wealth widens, due to the effects of compound interest.

The range of returns of the FTSE 100 doesn't narrow fast enough to overcome the exponential growth of the differences in returns between good and bad outcomes.

Assume that the difference between a good year and a bad year for the stock market is 20% (e.g. in a good year, the stock market rises 10% and in a bad year it drops 10%). If this range stays constant, then after 15 good years the investor has a portfolio that is worth about 20 times more than the investor who experienced 15 years of bad returns (Figure 1.6).

**Figure 1.6: The difference between a good and bad outcome increases over time**

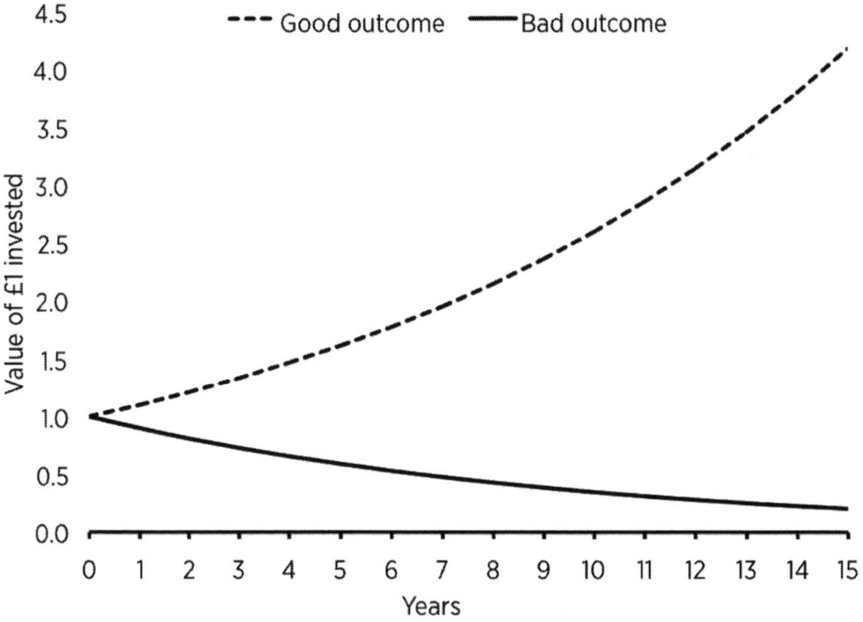

Source: Author's calculations.

If the uncertainty around the final wealth of the portfolio were to remain the same 20% after 15 years as it is after one year, then the range of returns would have to narrow from −10% to +10% after one year, to an extremely narrow band of −0.7% to +0.6%. The actual range of returns after 15 years is much larger than that and, as a result, the uncertainty about the future value of an investment portfolio increases over time.

The main thing to realise is that no matter how much market returns trend towards some long-term average, this is insufficient to overcome the increasing uncertainty around the ending wealth of an investment portfolio.

Now, let's add the fact that, in reality, investors are not dealing with past returns, but have to estimate future returns. As we have seen above, the estimation error around future returns increases as the investment horizon increases. This means that the range of estimated future returns of a stock market investment narrows at an even slower pace than observed in the past. The effect is again a competition between compound interest and a narrowing return range.

Any mistake in the forecast, even if it is small, will be compounded over time and act against the natural tendency of the range of returns to narrow. As a result, the range of possible final wealth of an investment portfolio will widen even more than shown in Figure 1.5.

This is exactly what Lubos Pastor and Robert Stambaugh of the University of Chicago found. Using a sophisticated model for how estimation errors and realised stock market returns interact over time, they found that the range of possible outcomes increases as the investment horizon increases. In other words, stocks – and all other investments – do get riskier, in terms of final wealth, and more uncertain as the investment horizon grows.

## More isn't more: information versus accuracy

A natural reaction to the realisation that the future is uncertain, and that forecasts typically have significant estimation errors, is to focus on and refine the details of the forecast. If forecasts of stock market returns are subject to sizeable estimation errors, then maybe their accuracy can be improved by estimating future company earnings and making some assumption about the trend for the price-to-earnings (PE) ratio. These two projections will then produce a forecast of return. Thus, by considering two other variables, a better forecast might be developed for the third variable.

This approach turns one forecast (stock market return) into two separate forecasts (one for earnings and one for the PE ratio). Digging deeper, earnings themselves can be forecast by forecasting sales growth and profit margins. Profit margins, in turn, depend on a forecast of inflation, fixed costs of a business, interest expenses, tax burdens, and on and on.

The hope is that as the analyst or investor becomes more granular, they start to understand the business better and can compensate for forecasting errors in other areas. For example, the investor may be overly optimistic about future sales growth, but pessimistic about profit margins. Combining the two to create an earnings forecast should lead to a more accurate forecast than any individual component. This is the approach of analysts and portfolio managers around the world, as well as that taken in the Geely report mentioned above. Yet, in my opinion, while this approach to forecasting is incredibly valuable, it is *not* able to increase the accuracy of forecasts.

# The true value of company analysis

Analysing a business in detail is a particularly valuable approach as it allows investors to understand how the company works, and what risks may be buried under the otherwise shiny surface. For example, a thorough examination of a business can uncover potential bottlenecks for future growth or areas that might lead to a cost explosion if the environment changes. This, in turn, helps the investor understand under what circumstances the profitability of the business might suffer. While it may be impossible to forecast how profitability will develop in the future, the investor can recognise trends to watch in order to get an early warning sign for future underperformance of the business.

In the most egregious cases, a thorough analysis can prevent investors from deploying money in a fraudulent business. Enron is a classic case study of this, where analysts who scrutinised the business simply could not understand how the company made money. Company management ridiculed these critics, stating publicly that these people simply did not understand the business. Many investors chose to believe Enron's claim, rather than the scepticism of a few analysts. In the end, it became clear that Enron was a fraudulent company and many investors lost their money when it finally went bankrupt in 2001.

The greatest investors of all time, like Benjamin Graham, Warren Buffett, Peter Lynch and John Templeton, may have had vastly different approaches to analysing businesses and identifying investment opportunities. Yet, no matter the investment philosophy, what differentiated this group from the rest of the investment crowd was their ability to analyse a business thoroughly and understand the risks and opportunities in each business. What they did not do, however, was try to summarise their insights into a single number, like a price target or an expected return.

The risks and opportunities of a business cannot be expressed by a single number, only by a range of potential outcomes. If that range was tilted more towards the risks than the opportunities, they would refrain from investing in that business, or sell existing investments. If the range was more tilted towards the opportunities than the risks, these people would invest in the business.

# Resist the temptation to summarise everything into one number

Of course, the temptation to distil all the hard work of analysing a business into a single forecast grows as the investor knows more and more about the business. Back in the 1960s, Stuart Oskamp gave 32 psychologists a patient case study and asked them to answer 25 questions, including some that required judgement about the personality of the patient.

The trick in Oskamp's study was to split the information about the case into four blocks. To begin with, the psychologists were given a limited amount of information about the patient before being asked to answer the 25 questions. In round two, they were given additional information before again answering the questions. This procedure was repeated twice more, each time giving the psychologists more information about the patient. After each round, Oskamp asked the psychologists to not only answer the questions about the patient, but also to predict how many questions they answered correctly. Figure 1.7 shows the result of his study.

**Figure 1.7: Estimated and true accuracy in psychological assessments**

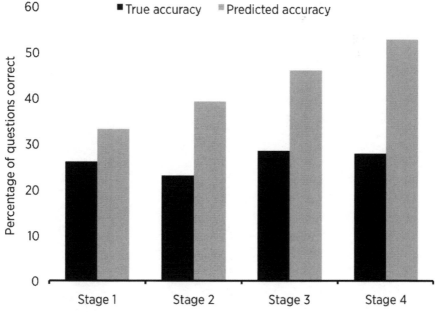

Source: Oskamp (1965).

After each round, the percentage of questions answered correctly was about 25%, yet, as they were given more information, the psychologists predicted they would answer more questions correctly. With every round they became more confident in their answers, even though the accuracy of their answers did not change. Oskamp reports that except for two psychologists, all participants were overconfident in their ability to answer the questions, i.e. they thought they had answered more questions correctly than they actually had.

Assessing the clinical profile of a patient is one thing, but stock markets or investments in general are something different altogether. After all, there is no way to measure personality or the degree of pain a patient is in with any objective accuracy, while businesses present a whole avalanche of numbers each quarter to provide investors with a measure of their prospects. With the help of these numbers it should be easier to forecast returns of a stock or any other investment, if not for laypeople then at least for professionals who are trained in financial statement analysis and can spend a lot of time investigating a business. Right?

Figure 1.8 shows the result of a study by Gustaf Törngren and Henry Montgomery. The study asked 43 stock market professionals and 63 laypeople to forecast the return of 20 different stocks over the subsequent month. Similarly, both groups were asked to give a forecast of the return, as well as the uncertainty around that forecast. Finally, they were asked how accurate they thought their own forecasts, as well as that of the other group, were going to be. The study had some astonishing results.

**Figure 1.8: Estimated and true accuracy in stock market predictions**

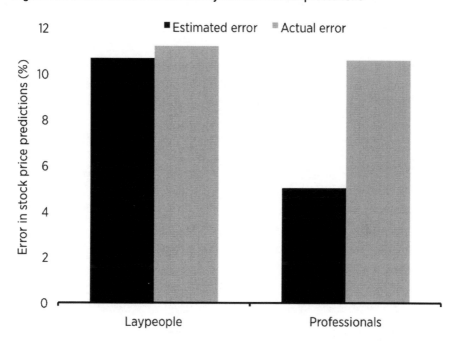

Source: Törngren and Montgomery (2004).

Both professionals and laypeople had about the same accuracy in their stock market predictions. In only about 40% of cases, the true return of the stock was within the range of the forecasts. While professionals forecast that their errors would be about half the size of their actual errors, laypeople were less confident and predicted an error rate roughly the same size as their actual errors. Funnily enough, laypeople thought that professionals would be much more accurate in their forecasts. Both professionals and laypeople expected the forecast error of professionals to be half the size of laypeople, while in practice it was about the same.

The researchers also investigated how professionals and laypeople made their forecasts. They reported that laypeople seemed to rely heavily on rules of thumb, while professionals relied on specific information about a company or a stock. However, professionals did not check the reliability and accuracy of this information and, hence, fell victim to a lack of analysis of the data they used. This is yet another example of why fundamental analysis is so important to generate performance. While it won't allow an investor to make better forecasts, it does prevent them from falling prey to unreliable or inaccurate information.

# Integrating uncertainty into the investment process

By now, I have – hopefully – convinced you of two things. First, that point forecasts, like target index levels in a year's time, are of little, if any, value for investors. Second, that the estimation error of any forecast in financial markets can be huge and should be incorporated into the investment process.

In order to improve their investment decisions and create better performing portfolios, investors should respect both of these insights and change their investment process in such a way that erroneous point forecasts and large estimation errors do not unduly damage the return of an otherwise good investment.

Tackling the issue of unreliable point forecasts is easy to solve in practice: just don't use them! At one stage in my career, I was managing three model portfolios for Swiss stocks, Eurozone stocks and British stocks for advisory clients at different wealth management institutions in Europe. I managed these portfolios with an investment approach that selected attractively valued companies with high-quality balance sheets and earnings.

One of the first steps in the process of picking these stocks was, of course, to identify a list of stocks that were attractively valued. This can be done in many different ways, but the most common approach is to use the PE ratio as a key metric. However, for reasons that I still cannot fully understand, most analysts use forward PE ratios, which divide the current share price by the expected company earnings per share over the next 12 months. Notice that this metric implicitly uses a point forecast for corporate earnings in a year's time. By picking stocks with a low forward PE ratio, the investor is implicitly accepting these forecasts as fact, and assumes that, on average, analyst predictions are correct. But, as we have seen above, analysts and strategists don't get it right very often.

When analysts forecast earnings, they must assess some companies that have strong earnings growth (e.g. technology companies) and others that have more docile and steady growth (e.g. food companies). Not only is the uncertainty around earnings forecasts of high-growth businesses larger, but, because analysts, like all humans, are overly optimistic, they tend to overestimate future earnings growth. As we have seen in this chapter, this over-optimism about future earnings is unlikely to disappear for professional analysts just because they know more about a company. Having a deeper and more detailed knowledge of a company only increases overconfidence and convinces the analyst that their assessment is correct, rather than reducing their over-optimism.

The effect of this over-optimism is that high-growth companies tend to have forward earnings that are more biased towards higher growth rates. Thus, forward PE ratios are more biased towards lower valuations. In other words, high-growth companies tend to look more attractive than they really are when using forward PE ratios, and analysts who use this metric are inadvertently introducing a growth bias into their value portfolios. This over-optimism about future growth in the case of high-growth businesses, also means that there is a higher chance that future growth will disappoint expectations. And missed earnings typically translates into negative share price returns.

These effects are the main reason why I decided to ignore forward PE ratios altogether in my investment process. Instead, I used trailing PE ratios as my preferred valuation metric, which divides the current share price by the actual earnings per share the company created over the preceding 12 months. Using trailing PE ratios to select stocks avoids the entire problem of forecasting errors and overly optimistic forecasts by analysts, but it also makes a crucial assumption: it assumes that last year's earnings are representative of the future.

This may sound like a heroic assumption, but remember the studies mentioned at the beginning of the chapter, conducted by Markus Spiwoks and his colleagues. These studies showed that you can beat analyst forecasts in almost all cases simply by assuming that interest rates, exchange rates and other market variables will be unchanged from where they are today in a year's time. If this is true for earnings as well, then using trailing PE ratios should prove better for performance than using forward PE ratios. And this is exactly what happens.

In Figure 1.9, I show the results of a backtest for stocks in four different regions between 1996 and 2016. In each region, I sorted the largest stocks in the market (the members of the leading market indices like the S&P 500 in the US or the Nikkei in Japan) by forward PE ratio and trailing PE ratio. Then, I invested in the cheapest 20% of stocks and measured their outperformance over the 20% most expensive stocks. The procedure was repeated on a monthly basis.

**Figure 1.9: Outperformance of cheapest 20% of stocks versus most expensive 20% of stocks**

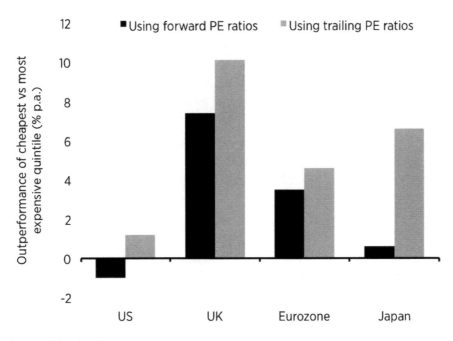

Source: Author's calculations.

Figure 1.9 shows that, in every region, the outperformance of the cheapest stocks over the most expensive stocks was larger when using trailing PE ratios, as opposed to forward PE ratios. In the case of the US, the result of using forward PE ratios even led to an underperformance of the cheap stocks versus the expensive stocks, which is absurd. What kind of a valuation metric leads to an outperformance of expensive shares over cheap shares over a time period of 20 years?

Using trailing PE ratios and ignoring forward PE ratios became a key component of my investment process while managing the three model portfolios I mentioned earlier. And while I also used a lot of other techniques, the annual outperformance of my portfolios over their benchmarks, of several percentage points after costs, showed me that ignoring analyst forecasts altogether was great for generating better investment results.

# A better way to deal with uncertainty

Ignoring unreliable point forecasts is one thing, but that still leaves investors with the question of how to protect a portfolio against the inevitable uncertainty that surrounds any investment.

A natural way to deal with this uncertainty about the future is to diversify a portfolio. After all, if you don't know what the future is going to bring, don't invest all your money into one stock or even a limited number of investments. This is old news, but diversification really is the best protection against unexpected outcomes. But it poses another question: if I want to diversify my money amongst, say, ten different investments, how much money should I put in each investment?

If I want to invest my money in stock market funds across ten countries, the outcome of choosing to invest 91% of my assets in US stocks and 1% in each of the other nine countries will be very different from a portfolio that invests 91% in Japanese stocks and 1% in each of the other nine countries. In both cases, the diversification benefits of the allocation to ten countries will not be able to reduce the concentration risk of putting 91% in one of the ten markets.

There are many ways to decide on the weight of each investment in a portfolio, but I suggest taking a step back and asking, what would I do if I knew absolutely nothing about the future? If I am completely ignorant about the future, I do not know if US stocks are going to outperform Japanese stocks, or whether technology stocks will outperform health care stocks. I do not even know if stocks will outperform bonds in the future.

Of course, in hindsight, it seems perfectly clear that US stocks outperformed Japanese stocks by a wide margin over the last couple of decades, and stocks outperformed bonds over the last century or so. We can incorporate this knowledge in a second step. But for now, let's assume I really am a know-nothing investor. In this case, the best way to allocate my money would be to put the same amount of money into every investment. This way, I spread my investments as evenly as possible, and make sure I will have a decent exposure to all my future winners – and of course a decent exposure to all my future losers as well.

When I ask investors what part of their portfolio they don't like, some tell me that they have no investments they don't like because they have all performed well. This is a red flag. In a well-diversified portfolio, you will always have investments that you hate because they lose money or underperform. That is the very nature of good diversification. Of course, in a well-diversified portfolio you will always have investments you love, too, because they generate high returns. If you did everything right, the winners will more than compensate for the losers.

In a ground-breaking study, Victor DeMiguel and his colleagues put this equal-weighted investment portfolio to the test by comparing its real-life performance with that of a wide range of portfolios created using typical optimisation methodologies. They found that, of the 14 different optimised portfolios tested, none could beat the equal-weighted portfolio. They even estimated that, for an optimised portfolio to outperform the equal-weighted portfolio, they would need 3,000 months (250 years) of data, if the portfolio invested in 25 different assets. Using a range of historical data less than that, the estimation error around future returns for the different assets simply overwhelms the diversification benefit, and a simple equal-weighted portfolio turns out to be superior. Most portfolios invest in way more than 25 different stocks and bonds though, and would therefore require thousands of years of data to overcome the estimation errors of future returns for the different assets.

The main challenge with an equal-weighted portfolio is that it is impossible to adjust the risk profile to suit different investors. If the same amount of money is put in every asset, the risk of the portfolio will be whatever it will be. If that risk happens to be too big for a given investor, then it is difficult to reduce this risk to an acceptable level.

One way to address this challenge is to assume we know something about the risk of the assets we invest in, but are ignorant about their future returns. For example, we can say with a high degree of confidence that stocks are more volatile than bonds and can expose investors to higher short-term losses. The optimal portfolio for a range of assets, where the investor knows the risk but knows nothing about their returns, is called a minimum variance portfolio. In this type of portfolio, all the assets are combined in such a way that the resulting portfolio has the lowest volatility possible. Just like their close relative, the risk parity portfolio, this low-risk portfolio performs about as well as an equal-weighted portfolio, and significantly outperforms traditional portfolios.

Furthermore, in practice, we are not completely ignorant about returns. While we are unlikely to know with a sufficient degree of confidence whether US stocks will outperform Japanese stocks in the future, or technology stocks outperform health care stocks, we have plenty of evidence that stocks outperform bonds in the long run, and that long-term bonds outperform money market investments, for example.

Hundreds of risk premia have been documented in academic studies and, while most of them are probably due to data mining or are so complex that they cannot be exploited by most investors, there are some cases where investing in certain types of assets (e.g. momentum stocks or value stocks) provides a systematic advantage. Obviously, we want to benefit from investing in assets that have an edge.

In these cases, we can try to incorporate this knowledge about future returns into the portfolio construction process, while at the same time reflecting the uncertainty of estimation errors as well. This is, however, where portfolio optimisation becomes more technical and difficult. The two best approaches I have come across are resampling techniques and Bayesian estimation of future returns.

The resampled efficient frontier technique, developed by Richard and Robert Michaud, essentially creates many different future paths for each asset in the portfolio by resampling past returns. For each future, the optimal portfolio is calculated using typical optimisation methods such as the mean-variance optimisation developed by Harry Markowitz. The average of all these individual portfolios is then used as the allocation for the asset.

In a Bayesian approach, a forecast of the return for each asset is combined with an explicit estimate of the estimation error. This estimation error then results in a higher expected volatility of each asset, which changes the allocation to the asset in the final portfolio. Both these approaches are mathematically more involved, but, in practice, they result in portfolios that vastly outperform traditional portfolios or typical benchmark indices.

For the vast majority of practical applications, however, a simple equal-weighted portfolio or a minimum variance portfolio will be fit for purpose and hard to beat, even by the most sophisticated optimisation approaches.

Finally, I want to stress that probably the best way to deal with uncertainty about the future is to be flexible. While marriage might last until death do us part, investments rarely last that long. Even Warren Buffett, who famously invests with an investment horizon of 'forever', is willing to cut an investment if the business is not able to live up to expectations, or if circumstances change.

Every investor needs to find a balance between hanging on to investments for the long run, so they can reach their full potential, and reacting to changing circumstances that materially impact the long-term outlook for future returns. Finding the right balance between these two contradictory requirements will be the subject of the next two chapters in this book.

# Main points

- Forecasts of interest rates, stock market returns and other important financial market variables are notoriously unreliable. Even the best professionals are no better than the flip of a coin when it comes to forecasting the direction of change, let alone the actual size of the return.

- In practice, assuming that interest rates, stock markets or exchange rates will be where they are today in one year's time is a better predictor than the consensus of individual forecasts.

- Estimation errors are substantial for investment horizons of one year, but they get even bigger for longer investment horizons. Mean reversion is not strong enough to overcome this growth in estimation errors.

- Analysing businesses or economies in more detail does not improve the quality of forecasts. It just makes analysts more overconfident in their forecasts.

- Nevertheless, there is value in fundamental analysis, because it helps investors identify risks and opportunities that have a material impact on the investment. But that is a far cry from being able to make better forecasts.

- Investors need to take this uncertainty about the future seriously if they want to improve their investment outcomes. One way to do this is to ignore point forecasts, like expected earnings, or to ignore future returns altogether. In stock portfolios, this can be done by ignoring forward PE ratios and other metrics that rely on forecasts in favour of trailing PE ratios and other metrics that do not. In broadly diversified portfolios, this can be done by investing equal amounts of money in each asset. Such equal-weighted portfolios are very hard to beat in practice.

# References

"Market predictions: 2019 to bring new level of uncertainty", *Financial Times* (7 December 2018).

V. DeMiguel, L. Garlappi and R. Uppal, 'Optimal versus naive diversification: How inefficient is the 1/N portfolio strategy?', *The Review of Financial Studies*, v.22 (5), p.1915–1953 (2009).

H. Markowitz, 'Portfolio selection', *The Journal of Finance*, v.7 (1), p.77–91 (1952).

R. O. Michaud and R. O. Michaud, *Efficient Asset Management – A Practical Guide to Stock Portfolio Optimization and Asset Allocation,* 2nd edition (Oxford University Press, 2008).

S. Oskamp, 'Overconfidence in case-study judgments', *Journal of Consulting Psychology*, v.29 (3), p.261–265 (1965).

L. Pastor and R. F. Stambaugh, 'Are stocks really less volatile in the long run?', *The Journal of Finance*, v.67 (2), p.431–478 (2012).

M. Spiwoks and O. Hein, 'Die Währungs-, Anleihen- und Aktienmarktprognosen des Zentrums für Europäische Wirtschaftsforschung: Eine empirische Untersuchung des Prognoseerfolges von 1995 bis 2004', *Wirt. Sozialstat. Archiv*, v.1, p.43–52 (2007).

M. Spiwoks, Z. Gubaydullina and O. Hein, 'Trapped in the Here and Now – New Insights into Financial Market Analyst Behavior', *Journal of Applied Finance & Banking*, v.5 (1), p.35–56 (2015).

G. Törngren and H. Montgomery, 'Worse than chance? Performance and confidence among professionals and laypeople in the stock market', *Journal of Behavioral Finance*, v.5 (3), p.148–153 (2004).

I. Welch and A. Goyal, 'A comprehensive look at the empirical performance of equity premium prediction', *The Review of Financial Studies*, v.21 (4), p.1455–1508 (2008).

# CHAPTER 2

## THE LONG TERM IS NOT THE SUM OF SHORT TERMS

Imagine you are managing a portfolio of stocks. As I live in the UK, let's take my portfolio of UK shares. I am a long-term investor and have an investment horizon of more than a decade for these investments. I have to file taxes, so I will have to check my portfolio at least once a year. This means that I will see if I have made a gain or a loss during the last year. Because stocks are volatile, I will experience a loss in my portfolio, on average, about once every four years. In the other three years, I will experience a gain. This feels good. Even though I have to file my taxes, checking my portfolio gives me pleasure because most of the time I have made money.

Just like everyone else, I like the feeling of seeing my portfolio rise in value and, just like everyone else, I am curious. So, I start to look at my portfolio not just once a year, but once a quarter. Again, because stocks fluctuate so much, checking my portfolio once every quarter means that I will see a negative performance for the quarter a little bit more often than once every year. A little more than one in every four quarters will show a loss. While I still experience gains more often than losses, I suddenly have to digest a loss during every year.

If I decide to check my portfolio even more frequently, the situation would get worse. If I check my portfolio every month, I will experience a monthly loss in my portfolio about five months of the year, and a gain only in the other seven months. If I check my portfolio every day, I will experience a loss on 120 trading days of the year, and a gain on 130 days of the year.

Did you notice how checking my portfolio more frequently shifts the odds of me experiencing a loss? If I check my portfolio annually, my chance of experiencing a loss is one-in-four. Checking the same portfolio every day increases the chance of experiencing a loss to one-in-two.

Now, ask yourself how you react if you experience a loss in your investments? Are you disappointed? Are you angry? Probably a mixture of both. But, most importantly, you will feel the urge to do something about it. You can't just sit there and do nothing. After all, you are losing money, and something needs to be done to make this stop.

Maybe you can hold still if you experience a loss in your portfolio once or twice a year, but if you witness your portfolio making a loss 120 times a year, the urge to sell something and buy something else in its place will become irresistible. Even though you are a long-term investor, you are suddenly managing your portfolio on a daily or monthly basis, shifting investments around in the hope of avoiding losers and picking winners. This happens when you focus on short-term fluctuations instead of long-term outcomes.

Short-term market fluctuations are fascinating and exciting. The financial media focuses on this volatility because, as we will see later in this chapter, it keeps us engaged and excited. We literally get high on financial market news. Whether it is the central bank hiking interest rates, the latest quarterly earnings report of a company or tensions in the Middle East, everything moves: stocks, bonds, currencies and commodities. Everything has the potential to impact your portfolio. Oftentimes, it seems that these events can have a long-lasting impact on your portfolio as well, because they might change the playing field. But, in reality, many of these events don't have a very strong impact after a few days.

I once watched an interview on TV where a journalist asked a supposed expert if a specific event mattered in the long run. His answer was that he focuses on the short term because the long term is defined by short-term outcomes. My reaction was to look at the Imperial Russian Bond hanging on my office wall. It paid a nice 5% interest every year for many years – until the Russian Revolution came along and Russia defaulted on its debt. The long term, in this case, was not the sum of the short term at all. And investors in stocks and bonds of companies and countries that have gone bankrupt have learned this lesson the hard way. From Argentina to Indonesia, from Enron to Parmalat, all have done well in the short term – until they didn't.

The short-term experience of an investor can be very different from the long-term outcome. In the short term, everything can feel fine for a long time (e.g. as a stock market bubble builds), just to collapse at the wrong moment and leave the investor with deep losses. Similarly, in the short term, things may look much worse than they really are, as I have shown with the example of checking my portfolio. This chapter will focus on the negative impact short-termism can have on long-term investments.

But, first, who is a long-term investor? I would say almost everyone. Institutional investors, such as pension funds, insurance companies and university endowments have to manage their assets in order to achieve goals that are decades in the future. Private investors, on the other hand, typically have to save for retirement, or finance their children's education; goals that are typically years, if not decades, in the future.

Yet, investors are increasingly managing their investments for the short term rather than the long term. Figure 2.1 shows that the average holding period of a stock has declined from about five to six years, in the early 1980s, to less than one year today. Why have investors become so short-term oriented when their true investment horizon has remained long term?

**Figure 2.1: Average holding period of stocks**

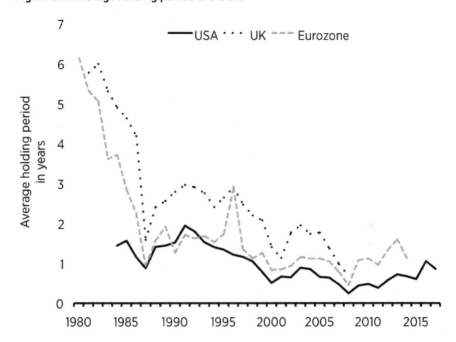

Source: World Federation of Exchanges.

## Let's blame the media, shall we?

When it comes to the rising short-termism of investors, there is a lot of blame that goes around. A common target is the internet and the financial media. With more and more data available at our fingertips, the competition between content providers has intensified and, with it, the media has had to dial it up to 11, as Spinal Tap would say.

If you watch CNBC, Bloomberg TV or any other financial TV station these days, there is a breaking news banner on the screen for the majority of the day, and a news alert seems to pop up several times a day. A hundred years ago, a financial news alert happened when people lined up in front of a building during a bank run. Today, all that is needed for a news alert is a central banker using the wrong words at a dinner speech.

The financial news media clearly has an increasing influence on market movements. Take, for example, the reaction of stock markets to an inverted yield curve (i.e. long-term interest rates are lower than short-term interest rates). A yield curve inversion has historically been a very good signal for a recession in about one to two years from the day the yield curve inverts. Historically, only financial professionals had access to the yields of short- and long-term government bonds required to notice a yield curve inversion. Thus, when the yield curve inverted, it typically took several days for the stock market to digest the news.

With the launch of CNBC in 1989, and Bloomberg TV in 1994, as well as the rise of the internet in the 1990s, this kind of information became instantly available to everyone. What's more, because financial news media must keep their viewers engaged, they were announcing an inversion of the yield curve as breaking news, ensuring that everyone who was watching understood what was happening in the markets, and what it meant for their investments.

Figure 2.2 shows how the market reaction to a yield curve inversion was quite unpredictable in the 1970s and 1980s but, with the advent of financial TV and the internet, became more and more homogenous, and increasingly negative, as more investors reacted to the 'bad news' of an upcoming recession. The only time the US stock market had a positive return on the day the yield curve inverted was in 1998, when the country was in the grip of the technology bubble of the late 1990s, and nothing was going to derail the relentless rise of those stocks.

**Figure 2.2: Market reaction to yield curve inversions**

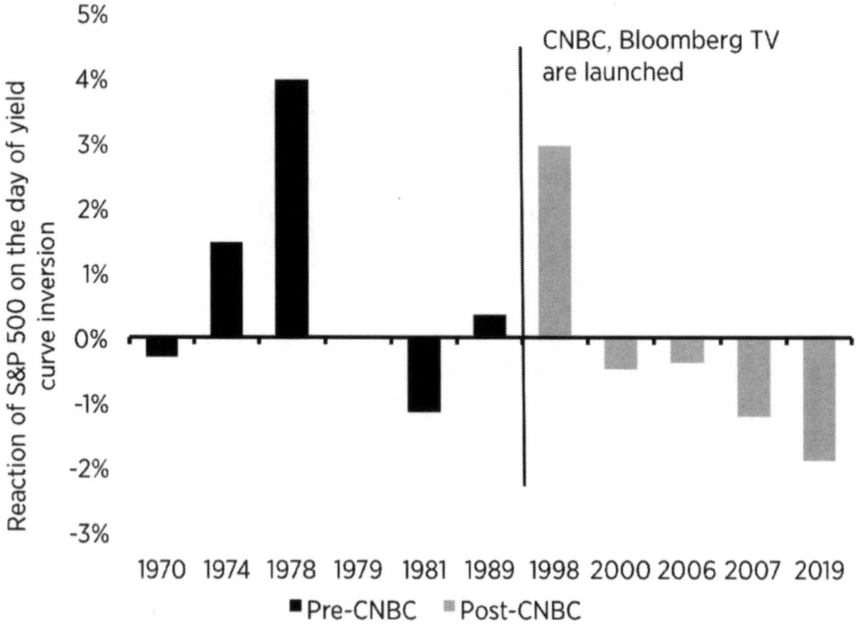

Source: Bloomberg, Author's calculations.

To ensure that all their viewers and readers understand the implications of an event like the inversion of the yield curve, financial news media relies heavily on the expert opinion of professional investors. And investors react to these expert opinions. Jeffrey Busse and Clifton Green analysed the market activity in individual stocks when a research analyst was interviewed about the company on CNBC. They found that stock prices react within seconds after being mentioned on CNBC, and trading volumes double in the first minute of the company being discussed. Positive news about the company is fully incorporated in the share price after just one minute.

A few years after their study, Paul Tetlock looked at the impact of a popular business column in the *The Wall Street Journal* and found that negative reporting about a company led to downward pressure on the share price of the company, and higher trading volume, in the days after the column was published.

Overall, it seems the media is at least partly to be blamed for pushing investors to trade based on short-term news.

## The media is a symptom, not the cause

In fairness to my friends at CNBC, *The Wall Street Journal*, and other financial news outlets, I don't think it is their fault that investors have become more short-term oriented in recent years. The media would not produce the content it does, if it would not trigger a reaction in their viewers and readers. Through a process of trial and error, media companies have learned what sells and what doesn't and, when it comes to financial markets, what sells is the anticipation of future gains.

To understand how deeply ingrained our lust for profits is, it is worthwhile to look at a neuroscientific study by Hans Breiter and his colleagues. They asked 12 people to participate in an investment game while their brains were scanned by a functional MRI (fMRI). The fMRI measures oxygen levels and blood flow in different brain regions and can thus give us a clue to which brain regions are most active when we invest.

One of the brain regions the researchers were interested in was the *nucleus accumbens*, a small area in each of the brain's hemispheres involved in producing dopamine, which triggers feelings of reward. The *nucleus accumbens*, and other brain regions involved in the so-called 'reward circuit' of the brain, are powerful forces that, when activated, make us feel happy and excited – giving us the drive and motivation to do things. This reward circuit is also stimulated by drugs like cocaine, as shown by Breiter in previous experiments with drug addicts, which enhance the drug's addictive nature. Because an activation of the *nucleus accumbens* is so pleasant, we can become addicted to whatever created that activation.

In their investment experiment, Breiter and his colleagues gave each participant $50 and put them in the fMRI. After two seconds, the participants were shown one of three types of investment. Each investment had three outcomes that were equally likely. The 'good' investment could provide the participants with a gain of $10, $2.50, or no change. The 'bad' investment would guarantee a loss of either $6, $1.50, or no change. The 'intermediate' investment could lead to either a gain of $2.50, a loss of $1.50, or no change.

The investments were shown after two seconds, but the actual outcome of the investment was shown after eight seconds. Thus, for six seconds, the participants were in a state of anticipation of future gains or losses. Figure 2.3 shows the activation of the *nucleus accumbens* during the experiment.

The fascinating result of their study is that the activation was highest not after the participants learned about their gains or losses, but during the six seconds before they knew the actual result of their investments. Furthermore, the participants were in a heightened state of excitement even when confronted with the bad investment that had a high chance of delivering a loss.

**Figure 2.3: Activation of the *nucleus accumbens* in anticipation of financial gain**

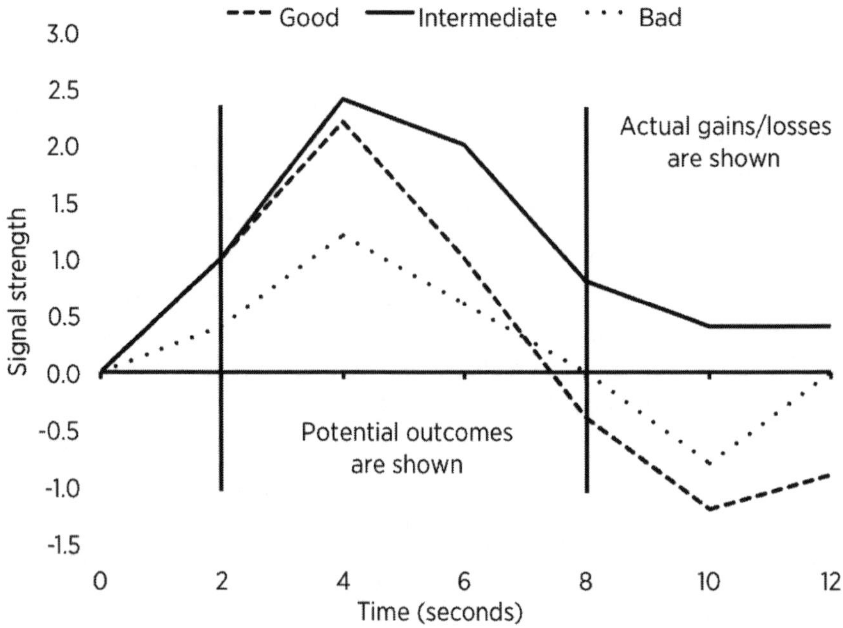

Source: Breiter et al. (2001).

What this and other experiments show is that investing is inherently addictive and activates the same brain regions that are activated by drugs. The excitement of investing does not come from making money, but from the anticipation of making money.

In my view, this is the fundamental reason why trading is so exciting, and why we tend to become short-term oriented as investors. Every time we buy an investment, our brain gets a little dopamine kick. Every time we get some news about one of our investments, our brain gets another dopamine kick as we anticipate the potential impact of this news on its performance. And as humans, we are programmed to do more of what gives us pleasure, so we seek out more news on our investments.

## Short-termism is bad for your wealth

Short-termism would not be so dangerous for investors were it not for the effect losses have on us. The example at the beginning of this chapter showed that if you check your portfolio more frequently, you experience losses more often. Thus, what happens when you check your performance is a small roller coaster of emotions.

First, the reward circuit in your brain gets activated and provides you with a jolt of dopamine as you start to look up the performance of your investments and anticipate a positive return. But the more often you look at the performance, the more likely it is that you will experience a loss. The first time you see a loss in your portfolio, you might shrug it off. The second time, you might get concerned, especially if you happened to have a loss in your portfolio the last time you checked. Finally, if you experience too many losses within a short time, or if your losses are very big, the parts of your brain responsible for feelings like fear and anger kick in.

Camelia Kuhnen and Brian Knutson have shown that, when we experience losses, brain regions responsible for emotions of fear – like the amygdala – are activated. This, in turn, triggers reactions of flight (sell everything) or fight (I have to talk to this manager and tell him what I think of his performance).

Figure 2.4 shows that even investment professionals are prone to such short-termism. It shows the results of a study of 3,400 US pension funds and their decisions to hire and fire investment managers.

The left-hand side of the chart shows the performance of the fired investment managers relative to their peer group in the years before they were fired. It also shows the performance of the newly hired investment managers before they were hired. The managers that were fired by the pension funds underperformed their peers over the two years before they were fired. Presumably, they were fired because they were performing poorly compared to other managers.

On the other hand, the managers that were hired instead performed extremely well in the years before they were hired. Thus, when confronted with underperformance, these professional investors fired the losing managers and hired winners instead.

**Figure 2.4: Performance of managers before and after being fired by pension plans**

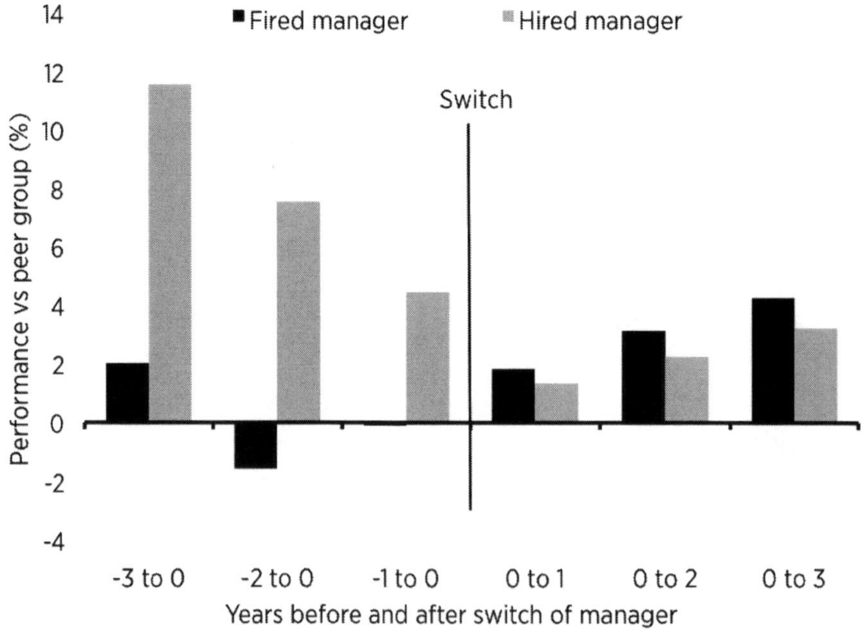

Source: Goyal and Wahal (2008).

The right-hand side of Figure 2.4, however, shows that the winners hired by the pension funds on average turned out to be anything but winners.

In the years after being hired by the pension funds, their performance was worse than the performance of the managers that were fired. Two to three years of underperformance may seem like a long time to many investors, and they can certainly feel long to an investment manager if he underperforms his peers and gets bombarded by questions from investors on a constant basis (trust me, I know), but it is certainly not enough to separate the good managers from the bad.

Taking investment decisions based on a few years of performance leads these pension funds to lose twice. First, they lock in the underperformance of the managers they decide to fire, and subsequently, they miss out on the outperformance of these managers as they recover from a spell of bad performance.

The situation gets worse if we look at investors who are even more short-term oriented than pension funds. In the late 1990s, during the frenzy of the tech bubble, Brad Barber and Terrance Odean got access to the investment portfolios of thousands of clients of a brokerage firm in the US. They analysed the trading behaviour of these retail investors, and the performance of their portfolios. Their findings have been published in a series of papers that have become some of the most famous findings in the investment literature of the last couple of decades. Financial planners and banks that promote long-term investment frequently cite their findings, though – strangely – brokerage firms that rely on commission income from trades rarely mention these results.

Figure 2.5 shows the return of traders relative to the overall stock market. The returns are split up by portfolio turnover, and reported before and after transaction costs and brokerage fees. The good news is that, on average, the investors had higher returns than the overall stock market. Even better, investors who were more active and had higher portfolio turnover tended to do better, before fees, than investors who were more passive. Thus, at least in their sample from the late 1990s, traders tended to add value by taking profits in one stock and buying another instead.

**Figure 2.5: Annual market-adjusted returns of traders**

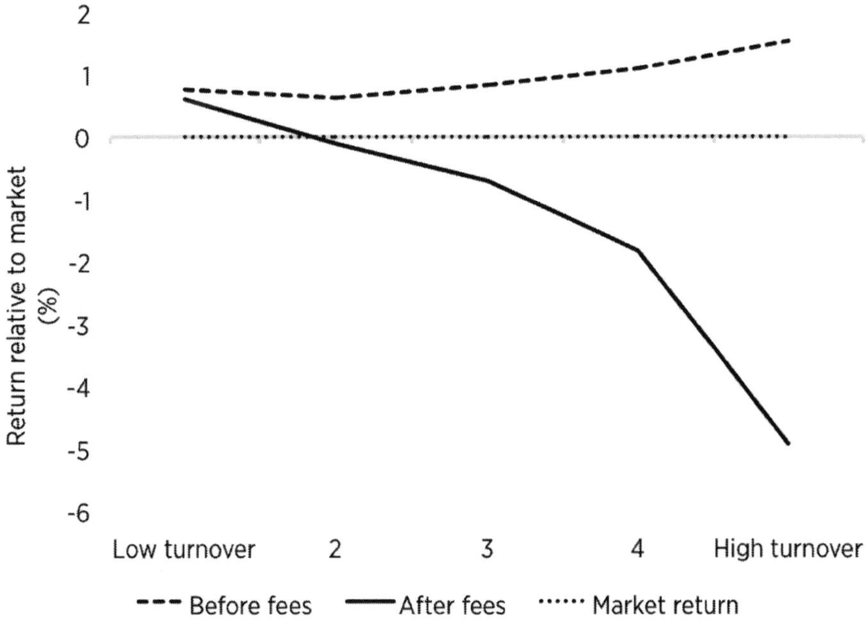

Source: Barber and Odean (2000).

However, once transaction costs and fees were taken into account, the picture looked much bleaker. Higher turnover was associated with rapidly declining returns simply because the transaction costs quickly ate up the returns, and more.

As a result, very active traders with high portfolio turnover underperformed the overall stock market by up to 5% per year, and underperformed the more passive investors by up to 6% per year. That kind of underperformance may not be too painful if stock markets increase by 10% to 20% each year, as they did during the tech bubble of the late 1990s. But in more normal times, the impact of these costs can be tremendous.

According to the *Credit Suisse Global Investment Returns Yearbook*, global stock markets averaged a return of 2.1% above inflation per year between 2000 and 2018. Therefore, stock markets underperforming by 5% per year in this environment mean losing roughly 3% after inflation.

As we can see, short-termism is bad for your wealth.

# Finding excuses for trading is easy

In my career, I have spent a lot of time advising private investors and I am always surprised by the fierce reactions that the studies of Barber and Odean can provoke in investors with a trading-oriented mindset.

Knowing the processes that are going on in our brains when we trade, those I have outlined above, I do understand why these people react so strongly to the data. It is like telling someone who consumes too much alcohol that they are an addict and need to get help. Hardly any alcoholics admit to having a problem at first. Instead, they argue fiercely that they have their alcohol consumption under control, and aren't like the other losers who are indeed addicts.

Admitting that you have a problem is the first step towards recovery, but usually this first step will only be taken once all other options have been exhausted.

In my experience, the arguments why a more active (trading-oriented) approach to investing is not harmful to performance go along several lines. The first line of argument is that the results may be true on average, but "I am different because my performance has been consistently good".

I cannot disprove such arguments of exceptionalism, but my advice is to run a simple test. If you are an investor who likes to trade stocks, then put a certain amount of your portfolio into an index fund that replicates your local equity market or the global equity market. This can be a relatively small amount for our purposes, since this account will act as a measuring stick for your performance.

The important thing is that you are not allowed to touch this investment for a whole year. With the rest of your portfolio you do whatever you normally do as a trader.

At the end of the year, measure the return of your portfolio (in percent not in dollars) and compare it to the return of the index fund. In my experience, this is a rather humbling experience for most people. If you are still inclined to argue that, this year, you just had a lot of bad luck, and that, over the long run, you would easily beat the index fund, then I suggest you repeat the same exercise the following year, the year after that, and so on.

The second argument I encounter is that Barber and Odean's results, shown in Figure 2.5, may be true, but the study was conducted in the late 1990s and is therefore outdated. Since then, investors have become better educated and have access to more information, which enables them to avoid the mistakes of overtrading.

Luckily, we can test that assertion, at least for the US. Because mutual funds and ETFs have to report flows in and out of their funds on a daily basis, we can calculate the investment return of the 'average investor' in a fund that reflects all the in- and out-flows, and compare this performance to the average performance of an investor who stayed put in the fund. Morningstar has calculated these return differences for several years and provides an update on an annual basis.

During the ten years ending on 31 March 2018, the company reports an underperformance of the average fund investor relative to the passive buy-and-hold investor of 1.4% per year. But the dispersion was large. For large-cap blend funds, the domain where most buy and hold investors can be found, the return gap was relatively small at 0.6% per year. For European stock funds, an asset class that, over the measured period, was rattled by the global financial crisis and the European debt crisis, the underperformance was 10.5% per year. These numbers show clearly that over the last ten years the underperformance of investors who traded in and out of funds was just as bad as the underperformance of the stock traders in the original studies from the 1990s. Nothing seems to have changed over the last two decades and if you think back about the neurological evidence I gave you on the thrill of short-term investing above, this shouldn't surprise you too much. Short-termism comes naturally to us and overcoming it is one of the most important things to learn as an investor.

Finally, the third argument I often hear from passionate traders is that since the 1990s transaction costs have declined dramatically. With the advent of online trading platforms, fees have declined to a small, almost symbolic fee that can hardly be relevant to overall performance.

As I have shown above, the returns gap remains alive and well in 2018, at least when we look at fund data. But Barber and Odean have done even better than that. Because their original study was done during the rise of online trading platforms, they could check the returns of the same investors before and after switching from a traditional brokerage account to an online account. Figure 2.6 shows their results.

**Figure 2.6: Annual market-adjusted returns of traders before and after switching to online trading**

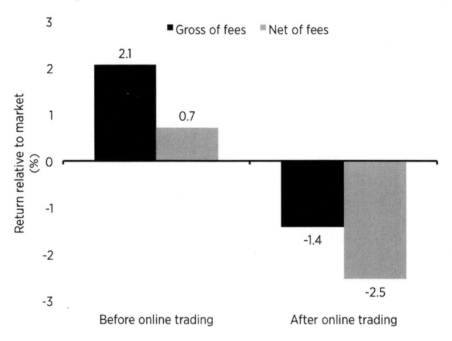

Source: Barber and Odean (2002).

After switching to an online platform with lower fees, the difference between the performance gross of fees and net of fees declined a little bit but, more importantly, the performance overall was much worse after switching from a traditional brokerage account to an online account.

I can only speculate about the reasons for this decline in performance, but my best guess is that with the switch to an online platform came greater accessibility to the short-term performance of the portfolio. Remember that in a traditional brokerage portfolio, you have to read your paper statement sent to you by the brokerage firm in order to check your performance. That typically only happens monthly or quarterly. Additionally, in order to trade you must instruct your brokerage firm by email or phone.

All of this takes time and presents a hurdle that must be overcome before a trade can be executed. In an online brokerage account, every bit of news is available instantaneously and trades can be executed with a few clicks. Furthermore, traders can observe their profits and losses on a minute-by-minute basis. More frequent updates on their performance mean that the temptation to trade increases and the news flow will provide a welcome excuse to do so. Instead, what investors should do is try to do nothing. Just sitting there and doing nothing is the first step to better performance as the next sections show.

# Don't just do something, sit there

If short-termism is such a terrible mistake, every action that increases the likelihood of taking long-term investment decisions should help improve performance. The problem with the long term is that it tends to be boring.

If you look at the chart of the stock market covering 20, 30, or more years, it looks like a smooth ride where meaningful swings happen only occasionally, while most of the time the chart just rises and rises. True, long-term investors also tend to be really boring people.

Imagine you go to a party and start talking to a chap at the bar. Turns out he is an avid investor, so you ask him what investments he can recommend. His reaction: "I bought Coca-Cola shares five years ago. Still own 'em." And with that the conversation ends. I know of fund managers who run some of the most successful funds in the world and they make one, maybe two, trades a year. Try to explain that to your investors.

Markets are full of uncertainties, from changing monetary policy to geopolitical risks, and the news channels are full of breaking news and news alerts on a daily basis. Your investors have trusted you with their money and you are doing… nothing? Don't they pay you for being active?

As I explain in Chapter 6, I want fund managers to be truly active, but that does not necessarily mean active in the sense of high turnover and lots of trading activity. Especially when markets are volatile, and things seem to go wrong, many investors fall prey to short-term activism. They invest based on the maxim: Don't just sit there, do something. Truly long-term investors often act based on the maxim: Don't just do something, sit there.

As we will see in the next chapter, this can lead to problems as well, if this long-term approach turns into stubbornness and an inability to change one's opinion when the facts change. But for now, let me explain how I manage to keep my focus on the long-term development of my portfolio, in the midst of all the chaos of short-term market fluctuations.

## Don't check your portfolio too often

In my view, one of the key techniques for avoiding short-termism in my investment decisions is to not check my portfolio too often. As I stated at the beginning of this chapter, I check my personal investments once a year when I fill out my tax forms. That's it. After that, I forget about my investments and check again in a year.

This may sound ridiculous, but I sleep very well at night, since I know my portfolio is designed to fit my long-term needs and give me the best chance of achieving these goals. If I check the performance of this portfolio only once a year, I increase the likelihood of experiencing a positive return, and that will inevitably excite me and prevent me from selling some investments in the heat of a short-term market decline.

Of course, not everyone will be investing exclusively for the long term. Some may have short-term positions alongside their long-term investments. In this case, I recommend splitting them up into separate accounts, so that if you check the short-term investments you don't accidentally check the performance of the long-term ones as well. Furthermore, by physically separating the short-term and long-term investments, you reduce the temptation to shift assets from one bucket to another – another potential investment mistake.

As a professional investor, I don't have the luxury to decide when my investors check the performance of my investments. But I tend to discourage them from checking performance more than once every quarter. Even so, I have had too many conversations with investors who complained about weak performance in one quarter or another.

The worst clients for me – and the ones that typically move on to another manager pretty quickly – were the investors that wanted to discuss performance on a monthly basis, and then became angry when they experienced a loss for a couple of months. These investors inevitably became caught up in the short-term gyrations of the market, and sooner or later were disappointed with their performance.

# Professionals need to have the right incentives

As we have seen earlier in this chapter, even long-term institutional investors, like pension funds, tend to assess their investment managers on too short a time frame. This leads to costly mistakes in hiring and firing managers.

A study by Linlin Ma and her colleagues looked at the internal incentive structures of fund managers at 5,000 US mutual funds. One of the criteria they looked at was the investment horizon used to evaluate fund managers by their employers. Many fund managers were evaluated based on rolling one- or two-year performance, though an increasing number of funds switched to rolling three-year performance. By now, a rolling three-year evaluation period has become best practice for fund companies.

Some fund management companies go beyond that and evaluate their fund managers based on rolling five-year performance, or even longer investment horizons. What Ma and her colleagues found is shown in Figure 2.7: the longer the evaluation period, the better the performance of the fund manager.

By evaluating performance over a period of five years or more, employers signalled to their fund managers that they should focus on the long term, rather than short-term outcomes. Given this focus on the long term in the evaluation (and presumably the compensation of the fund managers as well), managers made their investment decisions not with a view on recent market events, but with a focus on the true long-term prospects of an investment.

Investors who invest in mutual funds or delegate the management of some of their assets to outside managers would do well to learn from this research, and evaluate fund managers based on rolling five-year returns, or even longer time frames.

**Figure 2.7: Fund performance and manager evaluation period**

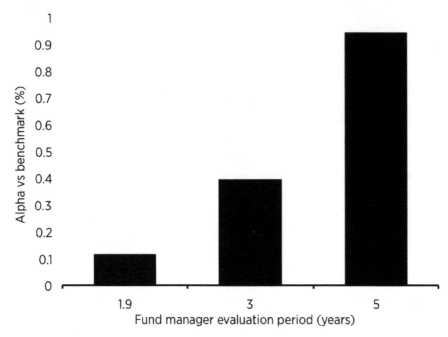

Source: Ma et al. (2018).

# How you visualise performance matters

A second technique for increasing the focus on long-term outcomes is to use visualisations that help contextualise short-term performance. Remember how I said that a long-term stock market chart looks rather boring? You can use this effect to your advantage.

Imagine you have a client who invests in a growth-oriented portfolio that is expected, in the long run, to achieve returns of 5% above inflation (Figure 2.8). A common practice of financial planners is to show the projected development of the value of such a portfolio over the next ten or 20 years, with a line showing the expected growth in value. A more sophisticated way of projecting the future development of a portfolio also plots a shaded area indicating the expected range that the actual value of the portfolio should lie in.

In the example below, I have used a 95% confidence interval. Only in the most extreme 5% of cases should the actual value of the portfolio lie outside the shaded area. This kind of chart is often used to show investors the likely range of outcomes of their investments. It is also an extremely useful chart for investors to estimate the likelihood of achieving their financial goals in the long run. But for some reason that I still cannot understand, I have never seen this chart being used to discuss actual performance over time.

Imagine, an investor monitors their growth portfolio on an annual basis (they are a sensible, long-term investor who listens to my advice). In year one, their portfolio has a return of 7.5%, in year two, 16.7%, and then, in year three, 10.7%. After three years, the investor is really happy with their performance, since they managed to beat inflation by way more than 5% per year.

In year four comes the first setback, with a return of 3.8%. Still, it is a positive return and, after the string of good returns, the investor is not too anxious. Year five then brings a massive bear market and the portfolio tanks by 31.3%. In one year, a third of the investor's lifetime savings are gone. Chances are, this is the point where they panic and become inclined to sell their investments or make some significant changes in order not to lose more money.

As an adviser, you would have a really hard time convincing this investor to stay the course, despite the fact they check their portfolio only once per year. And as an investor, you would have to muster all your self-discipline to *not* change your investment strategy and sell some, if not all, of the portfolio. What happened here is that the investor had a portfolio with a good chance of meeting their long-term financial goals, yet a single short-term event caused them enough panic to potentially abandon it. The investor might even have been educated about the range of possible outcomes in the long term, and still all this education and planning did little to help in the heat of the moment.

Now, imagine the performance of the portfolio was reported as annual returns, like we did above, but complemented by Figure 2.8. In this case, performance would always have been put in relation to the investor's long-term goals. After the first three years of strong performance, the chart would have shown an actual performance that was only slightly above the expected performance.

Furthermore, after three years, the actual performance line would have been very short compared to the overall projection. This would have shown the investor that, first, their strong performance in the first three years did not create a big buffer and, second, while three years may feel like a long time, it is a mere moment on the journey towards achieving long-term goals. Thus, after three years, the chart would likely have tempered their excitement over the strong performance of the portfolio.

Figure 2.8: An alternative way to show performance

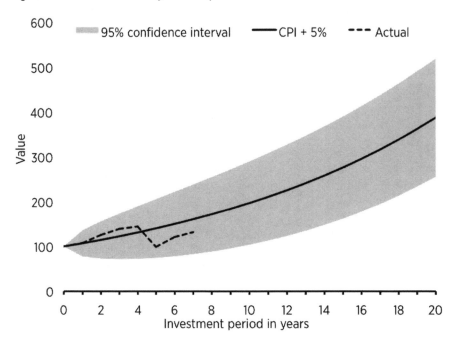

Source: Author's calculations.

After year five, however, the opposite would have happened. While the decline in the portfolio value by one third hurts in the short term, the chart shows that such a decline was completely within the realm of possibility. And even after the decline, the investor's actual portfolio value was still within the zone of portfolio values that could be expected from the outset.

Finally, though five years feel like a long time, the investor still has a lot of time to make up lost ground and reach their long-term goals. I am convinced that by putting the massive decline in year five into context like this, it would be much easier for the investor and adviser to leave the portfolio alone and stay the course. After which, the investor would have benefitted from the rebound in years six and seven that put them closer to the projected value after seven years.

In this scenario, the portfolio is still slightly below the goal of inflation plus 5% but, as our chart shows, this gap is small and there is still plenty of time to close the gap.

# Manage your information flow

The third technique to reduce short-termism in investment decisions is to slow down the information flow. This has two dimensions. First, it means reducing the amount of short-term financial data you consume. As we have seen in this chapter, it is very easy to access financial information on TV, the internet, or in newspapers and magazines. For your long-term investments, the vast majority of this information is not relevant. Thus, investors should try to limit their intake of unhealthy, short-term market information and instead switch to a healthier diet of relevant, well-reasoned analysis.

For professional investors, this means turning off the financial news channels streaming on every office TV these days. It also means shutting down Bloomberg for most of the day or, at least, closing the Bloomberg windows on your screen until they are actually needed for portfolio transactions. In my experience, good fund managers don't have to look at their Bloomberg screen all day long, once or twice a day is enough – unless of course you are a professional trader but, in that case, this entire chapter is irrelevant for you.

For private investors, this means turning off financial news channels and avoiding financial news websites. In fact, you should probably stay off the internet altogether and instead get the financial news exclusively from reputable print media like the *Financial Times* or *The Wall Street Journal*. Print journalism is in decline and deserves your support, so consider it an exercise in philanthropic giving, if you must, but please, when it comes to investing, stay off (most of) the internet and social media.

The reason I say this is because reading newspapers or other printed news not only filters out the quick takes and instant reactions to 'breaking news', which increases short-termism, but it also introduces a hurdle between getting the information and acting on it.

Remember the study by Barber and Odean, which showed that when traders switched from traditional accounts to internet brokerage accounts they increased their trading activity and had worse returns? If trading is too convenient and easily done with a few clicks, the risk of a snap judgement increases dramatically. If we have to go through several steps to execute a trade, our brain has enough time to deal with the dopamine rush and reflect on the news. Give yourself time to reflect before you act.

# Main points

- Financial markets and investors have become increasingly short-term oriented, even though most investors have goals that are long term in nature. The advent of the internet and financial news channels on TV have reinforced this short-term behaviour of investors.

- Brain research shows that we are getting a high from choosing investments independent of the actual outcome of our investment decisions. Thus, the more often we trade, the more we stimulate our brains. Trading can become addictive.

- Research shows that increased trading activity leads to lower performance after costs, making it harder to achieve our long-term goals.

- In order to foster more long-term oriented behaviour, and improve investment returns, we should evaluate our long-term investments infrequently. Generally speaking, we should check the performance of long-term investments only once a year, or once a quarter, and assess the performance of a fund or an investment manager only after five years or more.

- Investment performance should also be evaluated in the context of the long-term goals of the investment. This reduces the risk that short-term market fluctuations will lead to snap decisions to change the existing portfolio.

# References

B. M. Barber and T. Odean, 'Trading is hazardous to your wealth: The common stock investment performance of individual investors', *The Journal of Finance*, v.55 (2), p.773–805 (2000).

B. M. Barber and T. Odean, 'Online investors: Do the slow die first?', *The Review of Financial Studies*, v.15 (2), p.455–487 (2002).

H. C. Breiter, R. L. Gollub, R. M. Weisskoff, D. N. Kennedy, N. Makris, J. D. Berke, J. M. Goodman, H. L. Kantor, D. R. Gastfriend, J. P. Riorden, R. T. Mathew, B. R. Rosen and S. E. Hyman, 'Acute effects of cocaine on human brain activity and emotion', *Neuron*, v.19, p.591–611 (1997).

H. C. Breiter, I. Aharon, D. Kahneman, A. Dale and P. Shizgal, 'Functional imaging of neural responses to expectancy and experience of monetary gains and losses', *Neuron*, v.30, p.619–639 (2001).

J. A. Busse and T. C. Green, 'Market efficiency in real time', *Journal of Financial Economics*, v.65, p.415–437 (2002).

M. M. Carhart, 'On persistence in mutual fund performance', *The Journal of Finance*, v.52 (1), p.57–82 (1997).

E. Dimson, P. Marsh and M. Staunton, *Credit Suisse Global Investment Returns Yearbook 2019* (Credit Suisse, 2019).

A. Goyal and S. Wahal, 'The selection and termination of investment management firms by plan sponsors', *The Journal of Finance*, v.63 (4), p.1805–1847 (2008).

C. M. Kuhnen and B. Knutson, 'The neural basis of financial risk taking', *Neuron*, v.47, pp. 763–770 (2005).

L. Ma, Y. Tang and J. P. Gomez, 'Portfolio manager compensation in the US mutual fund industry', *The Journal of Finance* (2018).

R. Kinnel, 'Mind the Gap 2018', *Morningstar* (2018).

P. C. Tetlock, 'Giving content to investor sentiment: The role of media in the stock market', *The Journal of Finance*, 62:3, p.1139–1168 (2007).

# CHAPTER 3

# ARE YOU A LONG-TERM INVESTOR – OR JUST STUBBORN?

As we have seen in the last chapter, short-termism is a key risk to your long-term performance. In fact, I think that short-termism is the number one performance-killer for most private and professional investors. This is the reason why almost every financial planner and institutional investor in the world will tout the benefits of long-term investing.

I am no different. Not only am I a long-term investor, but I have a particular bias towards value investing and contrarian investing, two disciplines that require the investor to stay committed to a given investment over long time frames, often years. With these investment styles, the investment will often decline significantly before it recovers and lives up to its promise, so investors need to be prepared to hold on for the long run.

However, long-term investing can sometimes go very wrong as well; there are risks to performance from being the wrong kind of long-term investor. But, since I would never make such mistakes (or at least not publicly admit to them), let me tell you the story of a friend of mine.

Assume this friend of mine invested in the shares of a company that seemed extraordinarily good value. Nobody liked the business model of the company, and the consensus amongst investors was that the company would struggle to remain profitable in the face of rapid technological change. As a result, the valuation of the stock was very attractive and the expected future growth was low. The investment provided the holy grail of contrarian long-term opportunities: low valuation, a pessimistic growth outlook and shunned by the market.

So, my friend bought the shares and watched them… drop in price. Obviously, my friend, being the long-time investor that he is, did not panic. This had happened to him before and the investment case was solid. Then the shares dropped more, and then even more.

Figure 3.1 shows the percentage gain needed to recover a given loss in an investment. When the investment was down 10%, my friend needed an 11% rally in the share price to recover all his losses. When the investment was down 50%, he needed a 100% rally (or a doubling of the share price) to break-even. And when he finally had enough and sold the investment at an 80% loss, he needed a 400% rally to recover his losses.

To be sure, there are circumstances in which a company increases its share price by a factor of five, but these cases are like winning the lottery. Normally, to get to a 400% return requires not years but decades. And after all that waiting, my friend would still not have made any profits on his investment. Obviously, this was a long-term investment that went horribly wrong. But where was the mistake? Was it the contrarianism? Was it the value approach? Or was it something else?

**Figure 3.1: Percentage gains needed to recover losses**

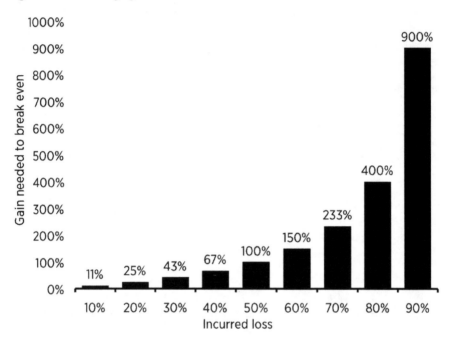

Source: Author's calculations.

# Contrarian investing for the long run

There are many ways to superior long-term investment performance. The simplest and, in most cases, best way is to invest in low-cost index funds and ETFs that replicate the performance of a given market, or asset class, and hold on to them for a long time. This will provide investors with the average return for these markets and asset classes and, if they hold on to these investments for many years, then the power of compound interest will grow their wealth exponentially over time.

In my personal investments, I have a core portfolio of index funds that are well diversified and allocated to different asset classes in such a way that I have a good chance of achieving my long-term investment goal of retirement security.

But, just like most investors, I am not content with average returns. I want to have above average returns and outperform the stock market with some of my investments. And I am overconfident enough in my abilities as an investor that I think I can do this by selecting single stocks or bonds, or specific themes in an asset class or market, that will give me superior performance in the long run.

These satellite investments are where things get interesting and require active management of my portfolio. The number one thing every investor has to realise is that if they want to generate superior performance, they have to take on a contrarian view to the market consensus in these investments. As the investment legend Howard Marks so succinctly put it: "You can't do the same thing as others do and expect to outperform."

This simple fact can be empirically verified. Investors know that the average actively-managed mutual fund underperforms its benchmark. Thus, if an investor buys the same stocks or bonds that most of the fund managers buy, he should expect to get a similar performance than the average fund manager; that is, a performance below the market average.

Figure 3.2 shows an analysis of the stock portfolios of 1,130 institutional investors from 1983 to 2004. These investments totalled more than $2trn. The researchers looked at the stocks and who owned them. Then, they grouped the stocks into different categories depending on how common it was for investors to buy these stocks into their portfolio, or how common it was for these stocks to be sold out of a portfolio. They tracked the performance of the stocks most commonly bought and sold.

Over the subsequent ten quarters, the stocks that were most commonly sold outperformed the most loved stocks by 18%. In other words, if you want to outperform the average institutional investor, just buy the stocks they are selling.

**Figure 3.2: Performance of shunned and loved stocks**

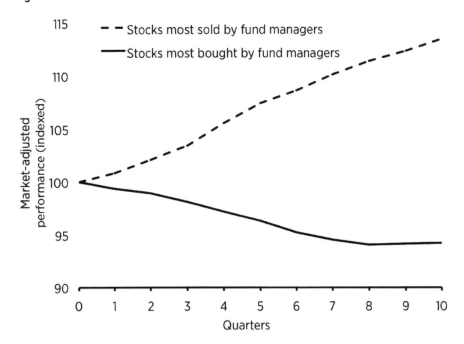

Source: Dasgupta et al. (2011).

# Contrarian investing versus momentum investing

Contrarian investing is hard because often it requires the investor to buy stocks or bonds that have gone down in price. This decline will have been the result of some fundamental reason, which is why many investors shun these stocks. Thus, contrarian investing often, though not always, equates to doing the opposite of a momentum investor.

Momentum investing is the domain of short-term investors and can be a highly successful strategy. In fact, momentum investing is one of the examples where – to use the terminology of the last chapter – the long term is indeed the sum of short terms. Momentum investing has been proven to be a reliable market factor that generates superior returns in the long run.

Yet, if we look at momentum funds, both in the mutual fund and hedge fund space, their performance relative to their benchmark, and after adjustments for size, style and other factors, is very low (Figure 3.3).

**Figure 3.3: Performance of contrarian and momentum funds**

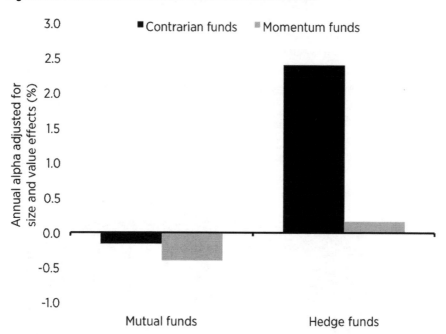

Source: Grinblatt et al. (2011).

In the case of momentum-driven mutual funds, they tend to underperform their benchmarks by 0.4% per year on average. I don't know exactly why the performance of momentum-driven funds is so poor when the academic research points to a significant outperformance of momentum stocks over the market in the long run, but I suspect it is a combination of too much trading (hence ramping up costs) and trying to overcomplicate the trading rules with additional quirks that eventually cost performance.

But, whatever the reason for the poor performance of momentum-driven funds, Figure 3.3 shows that contrarian funds outperform momentum-driven funds both in the mutual fund and hedge fund space. Thus, I conclude that it wasn't the contrarianism that cost my friend his performance.

# Value investing for the long run

Maybe it was the value approach that led to the significant underperformance of my friend? After all, value stocks can underperform growth stocks for a very long time. Figure 3.4 shows the length and size of the underperformance a value investor would have to endure if she bought the 20% cheapest stocks in the US stock market relative to the 20% most expensive stocks. On average, buying the 20% cheapest stocks would have outperformed the 20% most expensive stocks by close to 5% per year, but as the figure shows, there have been long periods of large underperformance.

**Figure 3.4: Periods of underperformance in value stocks**

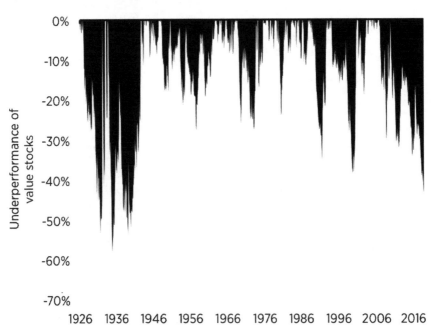

Source: K. French website.

If an investor had purchased the cheap stocks in 1927, he would have underperformed the expensive stocks pretty much all the way until 1944 and, at one point, his portfolio would have lagged by 58%. Similarly, value stocks have underperformed the most expensive stocks since 2007, and the underperformance has been as large as 43%.

In other words, it might take more than a decade for value stocks to show their superior performance. We know from the academic research of Campbell

Harvey and his colleagues that the outperformance of value stocks is real and above suspicion but, unfortunately, it is not consistent. There are long periods of massive outperformance of value stocks interspersed with equally long periods of underperformance.

On top of that there is the challenge that all investment styles face: how to define value. Just like there are many different approaches to momentum investing, there are many different approaches to value investing.

Amongst the most prominent valuation indicators is the PE ratio, where the price of a stock is divided by its earnings per share. Here, the discussion starts with the question of which earnings per share to use. Should we use the earnings of the last 12 months, which may not be a good indicator of future earnings? Or should we use the earnings per share that analysts expect to materialise in the next 12 months? As you might recollect, I am a strong advocate against using analyst estimates of future earnings and would only use earnings per share of the preceding (trailing) 12 months.

But there are other approaches to value. In the academic literature, value is often measured using the price-to-book ratio, where the price of a share is divided by its book value of common equity. This has the advantage of avoiding the embarrassing situation where a company loses money and earnings per share become negative. After all, what is a PE ratio of –10 supposed to mean?

Another approach to measuring value that has been popularised by Robert Shiller of Yale University is the Cyclically-adjusted PE ratio (CAPE). The idea behind this ratio is to divide the current price of a share by a long-term average of past earnings per share that spans an entire business cycle. This way, the investor averages out good times and bad times over a cycle, and gets a better understanding of the long-term average profits a company is able to generate.

Historically, the CAPE ratio can be traced back to the founder of value investing, Ben Graham, who used a seven-year average of past earnings per share. However, today, most investors follow the convention of Robert Shiller, who uses a ten-year average. Figure 3.5 shows the CAPE and PE ratios for the US stock market since 1979, as well as the long-term average for the PE ratio over those five decades, which is 17.5.

Looking at the figure, you can see how stock markets appeared very cheap in the late 1970s and early 1980s. Back then, the US was in the grip of runaway inflation and stocks had basically moved sideways for about a decade. Investors were so disillusioned that some people wondered if this was the death of stocks. Of course, it wasn't, and investors who purchased US stocks in the early 1980s would have enjoyed the longest and strongest bull market in history, culminating in the tech bubble of the late 1990s.

In 1999, both PE and CAPE ratios reached their highest valuation levels ever recorded. But it was only if you looked at the CAPE ratio that you could start to grasp the immense magnitude of the stock market bubble in the late 1990s. At levels above 40, the CAPE was more than twice as high than it had been on average over the previous hundred years.

When the tech bubble burst in 2000, and the global economy experienced a recession in 2001 and 2002, stock markets fell deep. The S&P 500 index in the US lost about half its value while the tech-heavy Nasdaq Composite Index dropped more than 80%. Remember Figure 3.1 above? When the S&P 500 was down 50%, an investor needed a 100% rally to recover their losses. Indeed, it took until May 2007 before the S&P 500 would surpass its highs of early 2000. The Nasdaq, on the other hand, would need a 400% rally to recover its losses, and it took until 2015 to surpass the high of 2000.

One of the reasons why the CAPE has become much more prominent as a valuation indicator in recent years is that, unlike the regular PE ratio, it warned investors of the financial crisis of 2008.

Figure 3.5 shows that, in 2007, the CAPE was still significantly elevated while the PE ratio had been hovering around its historic average for some years. The advantage that the CAPE had at that time was that it put less weight on the most recent earnings and more weight on the low earnings of the recession in the early 2000s. Thus, while the PE ratio was artificially low, due to the excessive and unsustainably high earnings of banks in the housing boom, the CAPE indicated that these high earnings would not be sustainable if a recession came. Investors who paid attention to the CAPE would have reduced their equity exposure before the financial crisis hit.

**Figure 3.5: US stock market valuation**

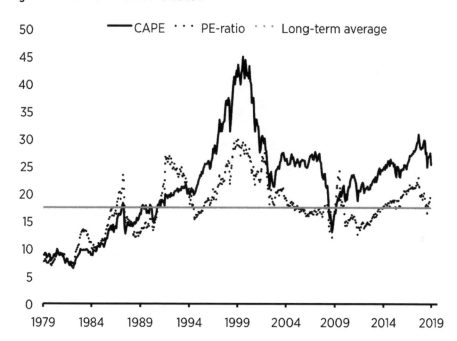

Source: Bloomberg.

# A cautionary tale

Figure 3.6 shows the performance and assets under management (AUM) of a US mutual fund run by an investor who paid attention to the high valuations of the CAPE before the financial crisis. This is a fund that invests in US stocks only and follows a long-term investment strategy that aims to outperform the market over a cycle or more.

In keeping with this long-term orientation, the manager uses the CAPE, and other long-term valuation measures, as a guide to his equity exposure. If the market seems overvalued, the manager tends to hedge the downside risks of equity investments to some degree, or, in extreme cases, completely (effectively turning the fund into a money market or equity market neutral fund).

If, on the other hand, markets seem cheap, the hedges are removed and the fund gets full exposure to US stocks.

**Figure 3.6: The danger of being too long-term oriented**

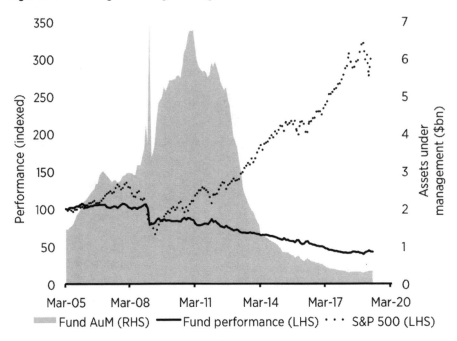

Source: Bloomberg.

Before the financial crisis, the fund was quite successful and had about $3bn AUM. And, while the fund lagged behind the S&P 500 in 2006 and 2007, the fund manager was vindicated in 2008 and 2009 when markets collapsed but the fund had only minimal losses. At the height of the financial crisis in early 2009, the fund had achieved its goal of outperforming the S&P 500 over a cycle. In the preceding five years, the stock market had gone all the way from the aftermath of a recent bust, to a boom, and back to bust again. Meanwhile, the fund avoided both the extreme boom and bust to create a much smoother ride.

This success by the fund manager did not go unnoticed and, in the aftermath of the financial crisis, the fund increased its AUM to almost $7bn. And the fund manager did exactly what he was supposed to do. He stuck with his proven long-term investment approach and looked at stock market valuation through the lens of the CAPE.

But look at Figure 3.5 again and the signal the CAPE sent since 2009. It was constantly in overvalued territory. Hence, the fund manager concluded that the stock market was still a risky investment and could experience another significant decline any moment. As a result, the fund manager kept the hedges and downside protection in his fund in place.

The result was devastating for the performance of the fund. In the ten years between March 2009 and March 2019, investors in the fund lost 52% of their investment, while the S&P 500 index gained 338%. No wonder investors eventually gave up on the fund manager and withdrew large amounts of assets. In March 2019, the assets under management of the fund had shrunk to just $326m – less than one twentieth of the assets at its peak.

To make matters worse, if the fund manager wants to catch up with the S&P 500, the market would have to drop by almost 90%, while his fund remained fully hedged and incurred no losses at all. This would be a decline bigger than any we have ever seen in the history of the S&P 500. Even during the Great Depression, the US stock market did not drop by that much.

## Learning from short-term investors

And this provides a clue to the mistake my friend from the beginning of the chapter made. The mistake wasn't with his contrarian investment position nor his value approach, it was his stubbornness. A long-term investment approach is highly recommendable, but there comes a point when losses in the interim become so large that it is virtually impossible to ever break-even again. If you then still stick to your investment, you are no longer a long-term investor, you are just stubborn.

Long-term investors – and especially value investors – like to look down on traders who allegedly 'trade on noise without a fundamental understanding of the investments they buy or sell'. Be that as it may, long-term investors can learn some important lessons from professional traders and other short-term investors.

First of all, traders tend to be agnostic about the reason why a stock or bond rises or falls. They buy a stock when they see additional demand for it in the market, or when the price momentum is up and looks like it is going to remain intact. They don't care if a stock climbs due to its attractive valuation, its great profits in the last quarter, or because it just announced a change in CEO.

They also don't care to find out why the stock, at some point, stops its climb. They couldn't care less, they just sell the stock, bag the gain, and move on to the next investment. Similarly, if a stock declines, they don't care why it does so, they just sell the stock and stay away from it, or they short the stock and hope to make a profit as the share price continues to decline. And at some point, they might reverse their position and buy the stock again but, until then, they don't really care what is driving the price.

Long-term investors, on the other hand, tend to follow an investment philosophy like value investing. This is the correct approach for them because, without a strategy, the risk is that the long-term investor will fall prey to short-term fluctuations – selling investments after a short-term setback or buying investments after a short-term bounce. In other words, for a long-term investor, the investment philosophy, and the strategy for implementing that philosophy, prevents them from falling prey to the temptations of short-termism.

But the problem is that there is no investment strategy that works all the time. As markets go through the ups and downs of a cycle, there are phases when momentum investing is the most successful approach, and phases when value or contrarian investing are more successful (Figure 3.7).

**Figure 3.7: Contrarians and momentum investors in the cycle**

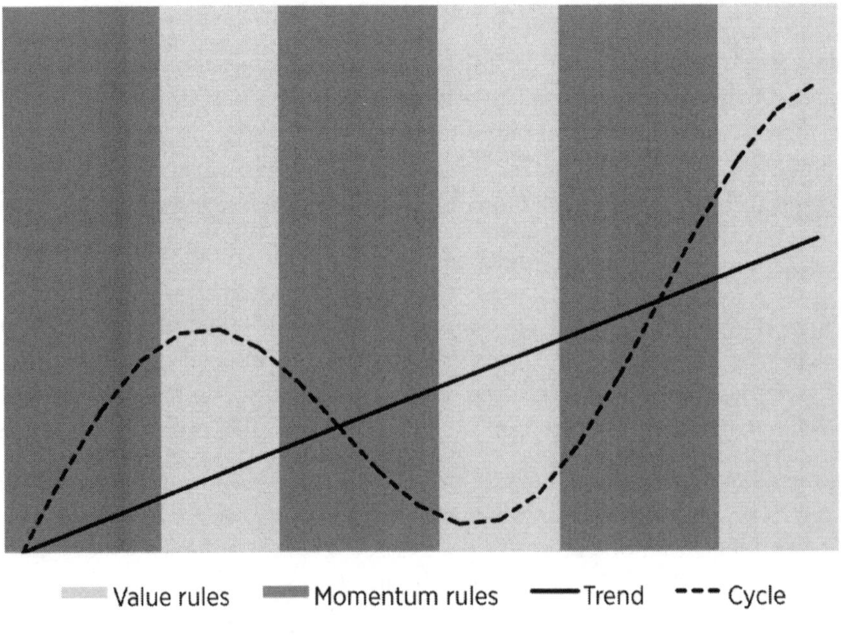

Value rules    Momentum rules    Trend    --- Cycle

Source: Author.

Many investors and academics have tried to figure out how to time the market and switch from momentum to value, and back again, in order to maximise the performance of their portfolio. But, after almost a hundred years of market research, there still seems to be no one who can time the market successfully. Keep this in mind the next time someone presents you with a strategy to time the market or suggests you switch from one investment to another in a systematic way to improve performance.

This person effectively makes the claim that he (or she, but mostly he) is smarter than all the legends of investing of the past. He is smarter than Warren Buffett and Peter Lynch, George Soros and Howard Marks, etc.

Most of the time, these market timing strategies have only a short history of successful performance when they are being sold. It is as if a 12-year old kid comes to you and says that he is faster than Usain Bolt was at that age and thus, when he has grown up, he will become the fastest sprinter of all time. Would you sponsor this kid for the next ten years or more in the hope that he will become the next Usain Bolt?

# The secret of successful traders: emotional detachment

Because there is no known way to time the market, long-term investors have to stick with their investment strategy for a long time – even if it temporarily stops working. And this is when human psychology comes into play.

The feeble-minded will abandon a successful long-term strategy too soon when it experiences temporary setbacks. The stubborn will keep holding on to a long-term strategy even if it has stopped working for so long that is has no reasonable chance of recovering.

In many cases, these investors become emotionally attached to their investments and their investment philosophy. They start defending it against all kinds of criticism, using ever more outlandish arguments why the investment has to turn around sooner rather than later.

What happens, in effect, is that the investment strategy slowly turns into a religion and a dogma. And dogmas cannot be questioned – it is often seen as heresy and, the more it is questioned by outsiders, the more the investor digs in. It effectively becomes a fight of us (the enlightened group of believers in strategy X) versus them (the heretics who claim that X does not work).

These dogmas are particularly prevalent in exotic niches of financial markets that are hard to value, or that have little history on which to assess the validity of the strategy. In the late 1990s, the dogma amongst tech stock investors was that technology would revolutionise the world and old valuation metrics were no longer valid.

In the early 2000s, the dogma was that house prices always go up. In recent years, the dogma has been that cryptocurrencies will replace traditional money. And an eternal favourite is the dogma that gold protects against inflation. All of these dogmas may be true in the long run, but as the famous saying goes: markets can stay irrational longer than you can stay solvent.

The second lesson long-term investors can learn from traders is the ability to stay emotionally disconnected from their investments and performance. Traders make dozens, if not hundreds, of investment decisions a day – many of which end in a loss. As a result, successful traders have learned to cut losses quickly and move on. The mantra of a successful trader is that cutting losses lets you live to fight another day. Stubborn long-term investors, like my friend at the beginning of this chapter, stay onboard the *Titanic* long after it hit the iceberg. They would prefer to sink and die with the ship rather than admit defeat and change tactics.

Admittedly, abandoning a sinking ship is very hard to do emotionally. In the early 2000s, Andrew Lo and Dmitry Repin wired up ten professional currency and fixed income traders as they were doing their normal jobs. They measured several physiological measures of stress and emotion like heart rate, blood pressure or the sweatiness of the palm of their hands.

Figure 3.8 shows the change in skin conductivity (i.e. the sweatiness of their skin) of experienced and inexperienced traders during large price jumps and trend reversals in the assets they were trading. The t-statistic indicates how significant the change in skin conductivity is. Experienced traders showed much lower levels of excitement and perspiration, they were extremely cool when compared to the less experienced traders. And in the case of a trend reversal, they even calmed down, while the inexperienced traders got more stressed.

When researchers looked at the performance of the traders, it turned out that the more experienced traders had better performance. Therefore, the ability to detach themselves emotionally from their investments and the market action contributed positively to their performance. If long-term investors can keep an emotional distance from their investments and their investment strategy, they can more easily tweak or abandon it when it has stopped working. In this way, they are less likely to fall prey to stubbornness and dogmatism.

Figure 3.8: Change in skin conductivity of traders

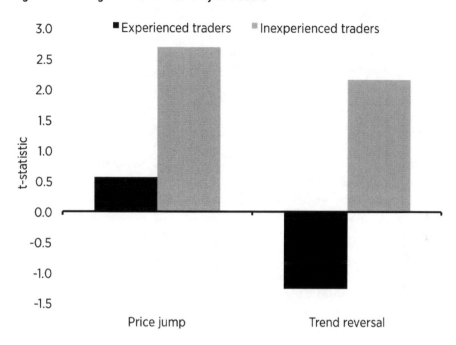

Source: Lo and Repin (2002).

# Listen to the data to rein in your emotions

In my view, the best investors are long-term investors that have an eclectic investment style – one that adopts best practices from other investors. Thus, if you are a long-term investor like me, you might want to think about how to learn from experienced traders and become less emotionally attached to your investments.

One way to keep emotions in check is through data. If an investor analyses a specific investment, they must look at all the available facts. That includes valuation, earnings, price momentum, investor sentiment, geopolitics, environmental risks, etc. The range is broad, and the influence the different factors exert on an investment changes over time. But, hey, this is why investing is so exciting. No two times are the same, so it is never boring.

Imagine you are thinking about investing in the shares of a well-established food company that has been around for many decades and is one of the leaders in the global food industry. Recently, trends in food consumption have changed, as many consumers want to eat healthier food that contain lower amounts of chemicals, additives, salt and fat. Furthermore, the rise of organic food provides an opportunity for the company to increase its profit margin. This would, however, also increase operational risks, since a food scandal could lead to a significant drop in profitability.

So, company management decides to transform the business to fit a healthier product shelf. Investments will be made into organic food production and the new trend towards plant-based meat-replacement products. In the existing convenience food products, like ready-made meals, management decides to change the recipe and reduce the amount of salt and fat. Simultaneously, the company decides to launch a new range of healthy convenience food. Because sugar taxes are introduced in more and more cities and countries around the world, the company also decides to put its division that makes soft drinks up for sale. How should you, a potential investor, assess this investment?

As a long-term investor you think about metrics that are relevant for the long-term performance of the shares first. For example, you look at the valuation of the stock and it turns out that, at a PE ratio of 18 and a CAPE of 20, it seems slightly expensive compared to its historical average. Yet, compared to other global food companies, it is relatively cheap.

The company has a history of being profitable even in the deepest recession and has never had to cut its dividend. Thus, it seems even if the company ramps up investments during its transformation, or if the economy slows down and drops into recession, the business should still be able to operate profitably and pay an attractive dividend.

Organic growth of the business has been meagre over the last five or so years, at a mere 3% per year, and profit margins have been relatively low. Chances are, if the turnaround in the business is successful, organic growth rates could accelerate to 5% and profit margins could increase substantially.

On the other hand, you know that the competitors of the food company are undergoing similar transformations, and, as you investigate, you find that the current management does not have a history of successful business transformations. Instead, they are a group of safe hands to manage the company in a solid and stable manner. Thus, it is unclear if management is committed to the transformation and, if so, if it will be successful.

Furthermore, the increase in sugar taxes around the world means that selling the soda business will be very hard. Potentially, the business will have to be sold at a much lower price than management thinks it is worth.

You can see that the picture is a mixed one. A value investor would likely consider an investment, as the company is valued attractively relative to similar companies and is not too expensive on an absolute basis. A traditional equity analyst, who looks predominantly at earnings growth, would likely endorse the investment as well, since chances are a successful transformation of the business would boost future growth and profitability.

A sentiment-driven investor would likely not invest in the stock because the management seems to have little credibility with investors, and the market will likely remain sceptical about the transformation for some time. And an activist hedge fund investor might be attracted by the valuation of the business, but may be uncertain if it is possible to sell the soda business and unlock hidden value in the company with the current management team.

In short, depending on your strategy, the stock is either a buy or a sell…

Being aware of these contradicting views is the first step to becoming a more successful long-term investor. If you decide to make the investment, the relative influence of these factors will change, and thus your assessment should change as well. The company may still be good value in a year or two, but if management bungles the business transformation and sinks billions into projects that ultimately don't become profitable, then all the value in the world will not help to turn around the share price. This might be a case when the investor has to cut their losses and abandon what seemed like an attractively valued position.

The big question is how to weigh the different viewpoints against each other. It is easy to say that after management bungled the business transformation that the stock should not be sold. Rather, an investor should hold on to stock until new management comes in, at which point market sentiment will flip and the share price should jump. But that moment may or may not come, and, when it finally arrives, the relief rally may be far weaker than expected.

# A mental model of data aggregation

My mental model for aggregating these different influences on a company's share price is to think of a ball on a billiard table (Figure 3.9). Unlike a normal billiard table, the ball is attached to the different sides of the table with rubber bands. These rubber bands have different lengths and strengths, and represent the different factors that can influence the share price. In the beginning, the ball rests on the table and does nothing. It just is attached to a few rubber bands.

**Figure 3.9: A mental model of the different drivers of investment performance**

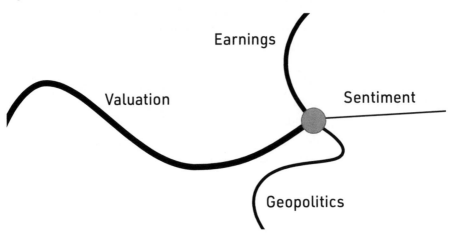

Source: Author.

Then, one of the rubber bands will be stretched and – as rubber bands tend to do – it tries to relax again, which gets the ball moving on the table. As the ball starts to move along the table it will start to stretch other rubber bands. Most of the time, the different rubber bands will not move the ball because they are relaxed or only a little bit stretched. However, in the situation I have described above, the rubber band symbolising market sentiment has stretched because the company management has just announced a corporate strategy that lacks credibility given their track record. This stretched rubber band will now start to influence the ball as it relaxes.

This movement of the ball will impact the other rubber bands and it is possible that as the sentiment rubber band relaxes, the earnings rubber band will become stretched. The earnings rubber band is thicker and stronger than the sentiment band and, thus, when it becomes stretched, it will change the direction of the ball.

In other words, as negative sentiment keeps dragging the share price lower, the outlook for future earnings growth may improve as company management delivers some first successes in the transformation of the business. Suddenly, the prospect of higher earnings growth drives the share price higher.

But, after a while, the earnings band may relax and another rubber band becomes stretched. The strongest and most influential rubber band of them all is the valuation of the company but, as you can see in our figure, as long as the valuation is not stretched (either extremely cheap or extremely expensive), it won't exert much of an influence on the direction of the ball.

This mental model of my investments has helped me, time and again, make sense of contradictory information. Furthermore, it helps me put my investment strategy, which remains driven by valuation considerations, into perspective. I can sometimes abandon a pure value strategy if I can identify other factors that pull the ball in another direction. Also, if an investment starts to lose money, the mental model helps me assess how long it might take before my initial investment rationally takes hold again, and valuation starts to drive the share price again.

# Embrace stop-losses

The second technique I have come to embrace, even though it is not part of the traditional toolset of long-term investors, is stop-losses. Traders and other short-term investors use stop-losses all the time to automatically sell a losing investment before it can cause too much damage in a portfolio. Long-term investors should embrace this simple risk management technique as well, because it can override the emotions of an investor and thus protect the portfolio when the investor may have already become too stubborn.

Data is not always able to override the emotions of an investor. Confirmation bias is our natural human tendency to discount information that contradicts our previously held beliefs, and overweight information that confirms our beliefs. I will talk more about confirmation bias and its impact on performance, as well as ways to overcome it, in Chapter 5.

Where to place a stop-loss?

The problem with stop-losses as part of your investment strategy, though, is that they might trigger at the worst possible moment in time, just before a recovery starts. Furthermore, what do you do after a stop-loss has triggered? When do you consider the investment again and think about a potential re-entry?

I have pondered these thoughts for a long time, and summarised my beliefs in an academic paper, but the main takeaway is, depending on your investment horizon, stop-losses should be set pretty wide for long-term investors, and narrow for short-term investors.

If you are a trader, a two or five percent drop in an investment might already trigger a stop-loss, since you are likely to make so many investments in a day or a week that even such small losses can quickly accumulate to a massive decline in wealth.

For a long-term investor, it is typically better to set stop-losses so far away that the typical short- to medium-term fluctuations of the market do not accidentally trigger the sale of an investment that might have turned out well in the long run. You only want to sell if the loss becomes material for your long-term portfolio strategy.

In my experience, there are two simple ways to place stop-losses: moving averages and drawdowns. The moving average strategy triggers a stop-loss once the price of an investment drops below a moving average of past prices. Traders might use 20-day or 5-day moving averages, while long-term investors are typically better off with a 200-day, or even a 400-day, moving average. These long-term averages typically only trigger a sale once an investment has already dropped significantly, but they can still prevent an investor from incurring devastating losses in the range of 20% or more.

The second approach to stop-losses, and the one that I have investigated in my paper and use myself, is to look at past performance and place stop-losses based on the asset's own price history.

As a long-term investor, you don't want to react to short-term fluctuations, so it is better to look at the longer-term trend. It turns out that looking back at performance over the last 12 months creates a long enough period to ignore short-term setbacks, but not too long to wait forever before triggering a stop-loss. Once the share price drops more than a certain amount over the last 12 months, it is safe to assume that the shares are in an extended downtrend that is unlikely to reverse soon.

Of course, the downtrend could just be part of a range-bound sideways movement, so the trigger for the stop-loss should be reasonably far away from the highs of the last 12 months. In my research, I found that, as a rule of thumb, a stop-loss is best placed at a decline of half a standard deviation below the high of the last 12 months. That sounds awfully technical, but what it means is that for stocks, which typically have standard deviation of around 20% per year, the stop-loss should be set at 10% below the peak of the last 12 months (or at 10% below the purchase price, if the stock was purchased less than 12 months ago). If the share price declines more than 10%, the position should automatically be sold.

While a 10% stop-loss is appropriate for equities, other investments with lower volatility require a stop-loss level that is closer. For emerging market bonds and high yield bonds, both of which have an annual standard deviation of returns around 7–10%, a stop-loss level at a 12-month decline of 4% to 5% makes sense. For corporate bonds, with their extremely low volatility of around 5%, a stop-loss level might be chosen as low as 2.5%.

To show how this works in practice take a look at the share price of Swiss food company Nestlé, a company that goes through a transformation process not unlike the one described for the hypothetical food company above. Figure

3.10 shows the share price of Nestlé in Swiss francs since the beginning of 2018, together with the drawdown from the most recent 12-month peak. As Nestlé went through its transformation process, the organic growth rate of the company dropped precipitously, which led to a decline in share price from its 2017 highs. On 6 February 2018, the drawdown reached the critical level of 10%, which is the stop-loss level I recommend for stock investments. At that point in time, investors were quite concerned about Nestlé and its growth outlook so, theoretically, the decline in share price could have gone on for much longer. In fact, throughout February and March the share price declined some 5% more from the levels that triggered the stop-loss.

The chart, however, also shows that in the case of Nestlé, the share price quickly recovered again and went on to perform strongly in 2018 and 2019. If we had just established a stop-loss rule without a re-entry rule, we would be quite mad by now because the stop-loss would have forced us to sell the shares and we would have missed out on a rally of more than 20% in the share price. Which is why I emphasise that if you have a stop-loss rule, you also need a re-entry rule.

**Figure 3.10: Stop-loss signal for Nestlé in 2018**

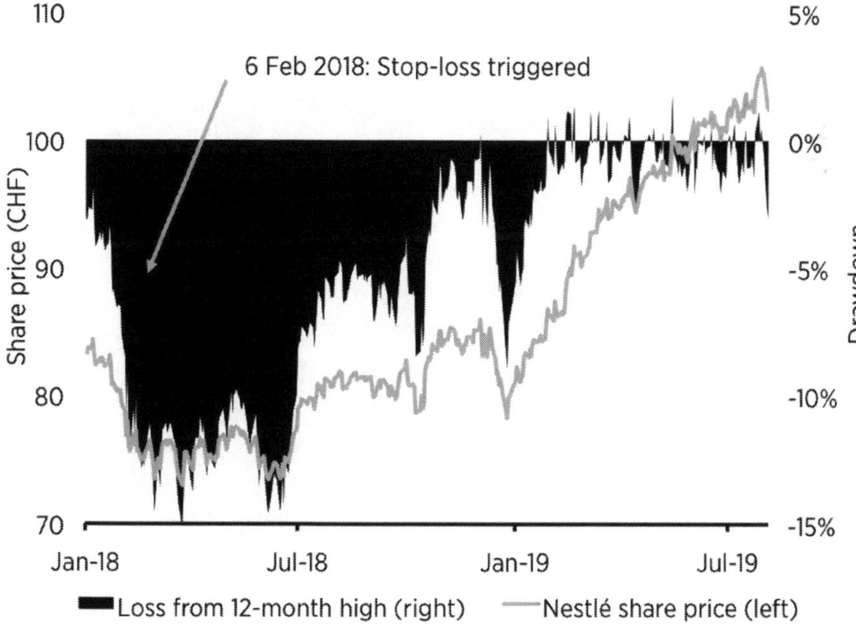

Source: Bloomberg, Author.

When to re-enter a position?

Once the stop-loss has been triggered and the investment sold, the question is what to do with the cash? If there are other investment opportunities, the investor might use the proceeds from the sale to invest in these opportunities. But, often, a long-term investor has put the stop-loss in place to avoid a broader market downturn.

If, for example, equity markets are hit by another global bear market, equities might decline by way more than 10%. After the tech bubble burst in 2000, and during the global financial crisis of 2008, equity markets declined on average by 40–50%. The goal of the stop-loss is to avoid such significant losses in the portfolio. But bear markets don't last forever and, at some point, the investor might want to buy the same investment again. Similarly, in the example of Nestlé above, the shares might eventually recover from their short-term losses and the investor might miss out on a substantial rally if there is no re-entry signal in place.

Even a casual glance at the history of financial markets teaches us that recoveries after a correction or bear market happen much faster than the preceding decline. Thus, if an investor used the same 12-month rule to decide whether or not to buy an investment again, they would typically miss out on much of the recovery after a correction. It is typically advantageous to set the re-entry signal for investments based on shorter-term performance.

In practice, I recommend entering a position again after the trailing three-month return has exceeded one quarter of the annual standard deviation of returns.

All this means is, for equities with their 20% standard deviation, the stop-loss signal should be set for a decline of more than 10% from its 12-month high, but the re-entry signal (i.e. the buy signal) should be set for a 5% recovery from its three-month low. This way, the investor only misses out on a small part of the recovery and re-invests pretty soon after a recovery has been established.

Figure 3.11 shows how this would have worked in the case of Nestlé. Once the investor has been stopped out in February and sold the shares, it is wise to continue to monitor the share price and look for a rally of 5% or more from the most recent 3-month bottom. After moving sideways for two months, the share price of Nestlé finally rallied more than 5% from its most recent bottom on 30 April 2018. This was when the investor would have bought the stock again. While the risk of a stronger decline in the shares of Nestlé would have been avoided, the investor bought back into the stock in time to benefit from the strong rally in the subsequent 12 to 18 months. In effect, the stop-loss signal in our example was triggered when Nestlé shares dropped below 76.90 francs and the re-entry signal was given at a share price of 76.98 francs. At the end of July 2019, the share price of Nestlé was 105.70 francs – a gain of 37.3% since re-entering the position.

**Figure 3.11: Re-entry signal for Nestlé in 2018**

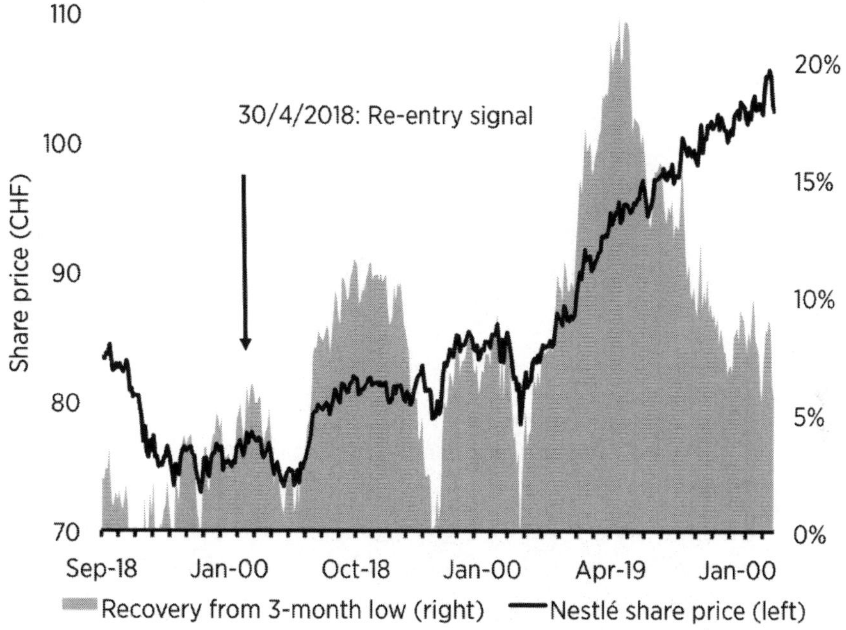

Source: Bloomberg, Author.

Table 3.1 provides an overview of typical stop-loss and re-entry levels that I use for my investments.

The combined effect of the stop-loss and re-entry rules is exactly what a long-term investor needs in terms of risk management. The stop-loss signal is a slow signal so the investment will not be sold based on some short-term setbacks, but only in the case of a severe price decline over a sustained period of time. But the re-entry signal is a fast signal, forcing the investor to buy the long-term investment pretty quickly after a recovery has been established.

Overall, the time in the market is maximised while the risks of large losses that cannot be recovered in the next couple of years is reduced. If I – sorry – my friend, had used this stop-loss and re-entry rule for the investment mentioned at the beginning of this chapter, he would not have held on to the investment until the price declined by 80%, but instead sold earlier and had an easier time to recover the incurred losses.

**Table 3.1: Recommended stop-loss and re-entry levels**

|  | Stop-loss below most recent 12-month high | Re-entry above most recent 3-month low |
|---|---|---|
| Investment grade bonds | 2.50% | 1.50% |
| High yield bonds | 4.00% | 2.00% |
| Emerging market bonds | 5.00% | 2.50% |
| REITs | 8.00% | 4.00% |
| Developed market bonds | 10.00% | 5.00% |
| Emerging market equities | 12.50% | 6.00% |
| Commodities | 12.50% | 6.00% |
| Gold | 12.50% | 6.00% |

Source: Author.

# Main points

- Long-term investing is the key to success for most investors. Hence, they should stick to a given investment strategy and philosophy over the long run and try to avoid reacting to short-term market swings.

- However, short-term losses can become so large that it is virtually impossible to recover from these losses within a few years or even a decade. Hanging on to investments with such steep losses is not a sign of a good long-term investor, but one of stubbornness.

- Investment styles like value investing and contrarian investing can be highly successful in the long run, but their returns come in lumps, and periods of underperformance can last for many years.

- In order to prevent excessive losses that are hard, if not impossible to recover, long-term investors should learn some techniques from short-term investors.

- These techniques should focus on emotionally detaching long-term investors from their investments. Emotional attachment to an investment can lead to an irrational stubbornness in the face of evidence contradictory to one's view.

- One such technique is to think about all the drivers of the price of an investment. While there are many drivers that can point in different directions, there is typically just one driver that is so extremely stretched that it will dominate the price action. Following how stretched the signals from different drivers are will help investors identify the direction of price movements in the near future.

- Stop-losses, combined with suitable re-entry rules, can take the emotion out of investment altogether, and are a helpful tool to prevent excessive losses while maximising the investor's time in the market.

# References

A. Dasgupta, A. Prat and M. Verardo, "Institutional trade persistence and long-term equity returns", *The Journal of Finance*, v.66 (2), p.635–653 (2011).

M. Grinblatt, G. Jostova, L. Petrasek and A. Philipov, "Style and skill: Hedge funds, mutual funds, and momentum", ssrn.com/abstract=2712050 (SSRN, 2016).

C. R. Harvey, Y. Liu and H. Zhu, "… and the cross-section of expected returns", *The Review of Financial Studies*, v.29 (1), p.5–68 (2016).

J. Klement, "Assessing Stop-Loss and Re-Entry Strategies", *The Journal of Trading*, v.8 (4), p.44–53 (2013).

J. Klement, "Dumb alpha", *CFA Institute Enterprising Investor Blog*, blogs. cfainstitute.org/investor/author/joachimklement (2015).

A. W. Lo and D. V. Repin, "The Psychophysiology of Real-Time Financial Risk Processing", *Journal of Cognitive Neuroscience*, v.14 (3), p.323–339 (2002).

H. Marks, *The Most Important Thing: Uncommon Sense for the Thoughtful Investor*, p.5 (Columbia University Press, 2011).

# CHAPTER 4

## WE LEARN FROM HISTORY THAT WE DO NOT LEARN FROM HISTORY

**A**s I become a middle-aged man, I must deal with a lot of changes in my life. For one, I have to face a receding hairline and a simultaneously expanding waistline. Along with these physical changes comes an enormous amount of investment in new clothes to accommodate my changing form. Unfortunately, clothes for middle-aged men seem to have a built-in invisibility cloak, since younger women somehow don't seem to notice me anymore – something that my wife appreciates more than I do. However, not all is bad as I approach middle age.

Especially in my career as an investor, I have become more relaxed and confident, because many market developments that would have increased my blood pressure in the past barely get my pulse going these days. My professional experience as an investor now spans two major stock market bubbles and crashes, as well as two global recessions and easily a dozen or so major sovereign defaults. I remember the days when Germans paid with Deutschmark and not euro, and when fraudulent managers at Enron went to jail for their deeds. I have seen government bond yields become negative in some countries – like Switzerland – for maturities up to 30 years and more.

Of course, this experience as an investor, together with the many other experiences in my life, inform my investment decisions and change my behaviour. Grumpy old men like me tend to be more cautious when it comes to embracing the latest trend in financial markets. After all, we have seen these trends turn into bubbles and then crash and burn a couple of times before.

On the other hand, grumpy old men are not just cynics who don't believe in progress, they can teach younger investors a thing or two about how not to panic when markets crash, and how to manage risks so as not to get wiped out if an investment goes wrong.

Robin Greenwood and Stefan Nagel have documented how experience influences the investment behaviour of professional fund managers. They looked at the performance of US equity fund managers from 1998 to 2002.

During the first two years of this time period, US stock markets were in the grip of the technology mania that led to the most expensive stock market valuations in history. Investors were chasing any stock that was involved in technology, media or telecommunication and stood to benefit from the revolution the internet and other new forms of technology promised. The excesses of this bubble are well documented, but one anecdote might be helpful for my younger readers who did not experience it.

On 29 March 1999, Computer Literacy Inc. changed its name to fatbrain.com. On the day before the name change was announced, the information leaked and the share price of the company jumped 33%. Nothing about the business or its prospects had changed. All the company did was put .com into its name and the stock rallied by one third.

The tech bubble eventually burst in early 2000, and from 2000 to 2002 – the second half of the observation period of Greenwood and Nagel – stocks declined steadily, with many of the high-flying tech companies becoming worthless.

What Greenwood and Nagel did in their study was to investigate the performance of fund managers in the run-up to the tech bubble, and once the bubble had burst. They further split the performance by the age of the fund manager (Figure 4.1). The results showed something interesting.

**Figure 4.1: The different investment behaviours of experienced and inexperienced investors**

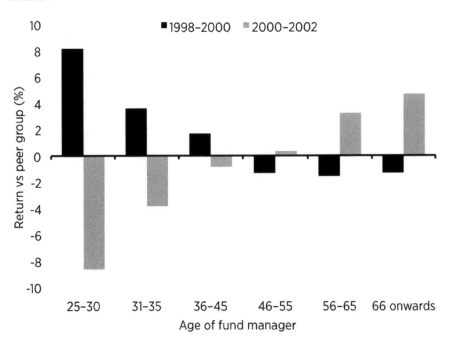

Source: Greenwood and Nagel (2009).

Younger fund managers were more willing to embrace the promise of the new technologies and invested more heavily into these stocks. As a result, their performance during the tech bubble tended to be better than the average of all fund managers in the sample. The younger the fund managers were, the bigger their outperformance in the late 1990s, simply because they invested more heavily into technology stocks.

Older fund managers, on the other hand, were more cynical towards these new technology stocks and invested less money in what they perceived as an overvalued sector. As a result, their performance during the late 1990s lagged behind the peer group average.

Once the tech bubble burst, however, the picture changed. Now the more experienced investors, who had refrained from going all in with technology stocks, outperformed their peers, while the younger portfolio managers underperformed significantly. Because the younger fund managers did not have first-hand experience with a stock market bubble, they held on to technology stocks for too long, even after the bubble burst.

Because of the differences in experience, the returns of older and younger fund managers differed across this cycle of bull and bear market. As a member of the more experienced group of investors, I wish I could tell you that in the end, the older, more experienced fund managers outperformed the younger ones. In their study, Greenwood and Nagel found a small outperformance over the entire four-year cycle by the more experienced fund managers, but that outperformance was so small that it could well have been due to chance.

This finding will become the red thread for this chapter. Our experiences have a significant influence on our investment decisions, but most people do not become better investors over time. The majority of investors do not learn from past experiences and thus do not improve performance over time.

This is sad and points to a crucial mistake many investors make. Our experiences as investors provide a treasure trove of lessons that can make us better investors and improve our performance, if only we take the time to heed these lessons.

At the end of this chapter I will give examples of two techniques I use in my investment process to systematically learn from past experiences, with the goal of enhancing my performance over time.

Before we get to these techniques, we first have to understand how experiences shape the investment decision of millions of investors around the world, and how the aggregate of these millions of individual decisions influence financial markets overall. This journey starts with us leaving financial markets behind and entering the laboratory of Vernon Smith.

# Learning from experience in a laboratory

Vernon Smith was a professor of economics and law at George Mason University in the US. He pioneered the field of experimental economics. In his laboratory, he created simplified financial markets and asked volunteers to trade in securities that were designed to have specific characteristics. Through his experiments, he and his colleagues could identify how bubbles and crashes, as well as other market phenomena, formed.

For his work, Vernon Smith, together with Daniel Kahneman, was awarded the 2002 Nobel Prize in Economic Sciences. But while Kahneman has become an economics superstar, I still have to explain to people who Vernon Smith is. Some of Smith's most important research was done on stock market bubbles and crashes. In experiments throughout the 1980s and 1990s, he and his collaborators showed under what conditions bubbles can form, and what role personal experiences of investors play in this process. To keep things simple, I will focus on the more recent research Smith conducted, together with Reshmaan Hussam and David Porter.

Imagine you volunteered to participate in a laboratory experiment on stock markets. As you enter the laboratory, you are invited to sit in front of a computer screen. On the screen, you see data from a simple stock market. The market has only one stock to trade. In every round of this experiment, the stock will pay a dividend that is randomly chosen to be zero, eight cents, 28 cents or 60 cents.

You know that the experiment will stop after 15 rounds, when the stock will become worthless. You are given a certain amount of cash and a few shares to begin with, and you are informed that there are 69 people just like you in the laboratory also participating in this market.

At the beginning of each round, you can choose to buy some shares from other investors, or sell your shares to other investors and bank the proceeds in cash. You have two minutes to buy or sell your shares. Then, the dividend per share will be randomly drawn from the four options mentioned above and you receive the dividend payment for each share you own. This completes round one. The experiment continues for a total of 15 rounds and you should try to make as much money as possible.

In the first experiments run in the laboratory, Smith asked finance students to participate. Finance students at George Mason University are not stupid, and they know how to calculate the expected value of the shares. Because there are four possible dividends, and each dividend is equally likely, the share is worth the average dividend per round times the number of rounds.

In our example, the average dividend per share is 24 cents and, thus, the fair share price would be 24 cents if the experiment were played for just one round. If the experiment is played for two rounds, the fair share price at the beginning of the experiment would be 48 cents (24 cents for round one and 24 cents for round two). Since the experiment consists of fifteen rounds, the fair share price in the first round is 360 cents (15 × 24), and then declines by 24 cents in each round (Figure 4.2).

**Figure 4.2: Fundamental value of an asset in the laboratory**

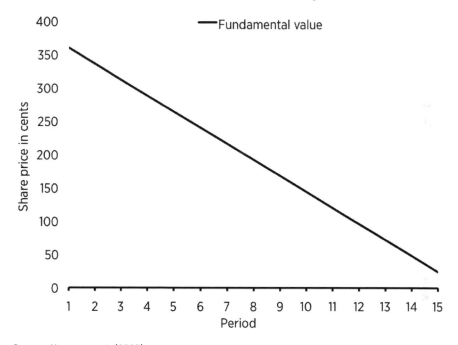

Source: Hussam et al. (2008).

# Trading begins and chaos ensues...

When the researchers let the students trade with each other, the experiments often seemed to go horribly wrong. The dashed, inexperienced line in Figure 4.3 shows a typical price path of the shares when inexperienced students traded with each other. The share price often had absolutely nothing to do with the fundamental value.

In round 10, the fair share price for rational investors is 144 cents, but shares traded at 468.3 cents – an overvaluation of 325%! The students had created a stock market bubble. This was no coincidence. In these experimental stock markets, bubbles appeared regularly only to burst as the experiment came to a close, and everyone realised the shares would become worthless soon. In the example in

Figure 4.3, the inexperienced line shows that the share price crashed by 90% between round 10 and round 15.

**Figure 4.3: A bubble forms in an experimental asset market**

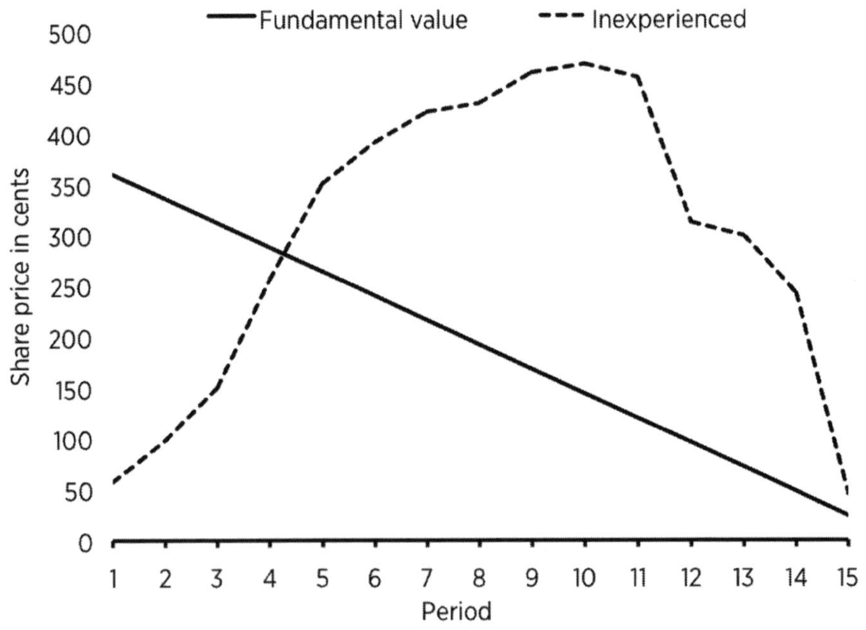

Source: Hussam et al. (2008).

The researchers first thought that the students didn't understand the task at hand, so they repeated the experiment with investment professionals. But that yielded similar results. Bubbles happened often, and were usually very large. What happened was that, instead of trying to pay a fair price for the shares, some investors were betting on the random dividend to be at the high end of the spectrum, and bid up the price for the shares in each round. More cautious investors were only too willing to sell their shares to these optimistic investors and cash in a capital gain.

Over time, shares moved from the more pessimistic, or more cautious, investors to the more optimistic investors, and finally to the most euphoric investors in the group. Eventually, there was no one left to buy the shares at even higher prices and the bubble burst. If this sounds familiar, it's because this is one of the most common mechanisms for how a stock market bubble is fuelled in real life financial markets.

However, if volunteers participated in the experiment again, they learned from experience and, after a while, avoided market bubbles. The 'twice experienced' line in Figure 4.4 shows a typical development of the share price in the experiment if it was played with volunteers who had participated in the experiment twice before. There are hardly any deviations from the fundamental value anymore.[1]

**Figure 4.4: Experience helps to avoid bubbles**

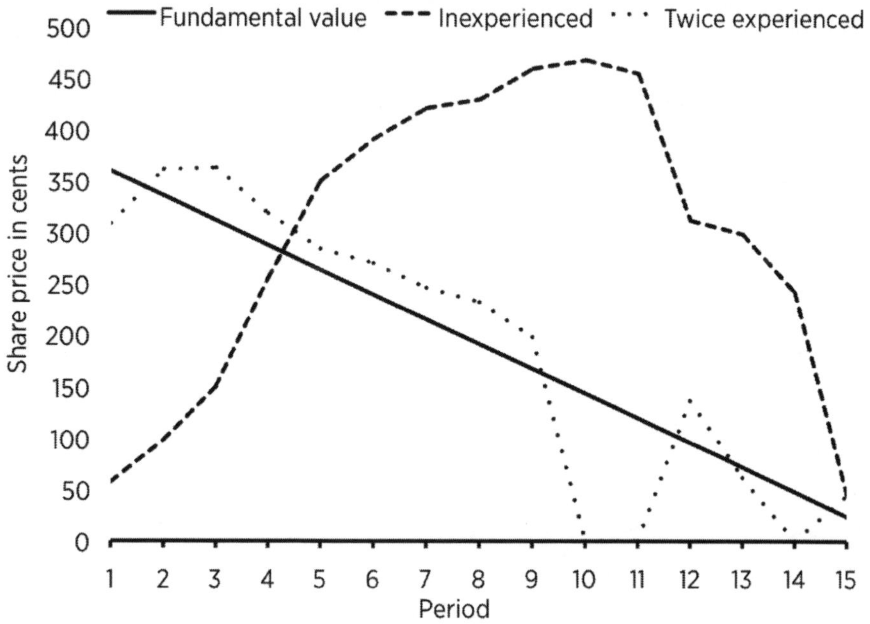

Source: Hussam et al. (2008).

# Cynical bubbles and bubble echoes

Note that this boring stock market, where share prices closely follow the fundamental value, materialised only after volunteers had participated *twice* before. When the volunteers had experienced a bubble once, and were then asked to participate in the experiment again, something strange happened.

The 'once experienced' line in Figure 4.5 shows a typical share price development when volunteers participated for the second time. There was another bubble!

---

1   In rounds 10, 11 and 14 in this experiment, the share price is given as zero. This just means that, in these rounds, no shares were traded, rather than that market participants thought the shares had become worthless.

The bubble in the share price tended to be similar in size to the first run of the experiment, which is odd, because it seemed that investors did not learn anything from their bad experience.

When the researchers interviewed the volunteers, they found that this assumption was not true. The participants had learned something, namely that there are enough 'suckers' out there willing to buy shares at egregious prices. Thus, the volunteers created a cynical bubble where they knew full well that shares were overpriced, but they hoped to be able to unload their shares to some unsuspecting investors before a market crash. Of course, that does not work and, in the end, many volunteers got burned a second time. That's when they learned a lesson and refrained from bidding stocks up above their fair value.

**Figure 4.5: The strange bubble formed by participants who had experienced a bubble once before**

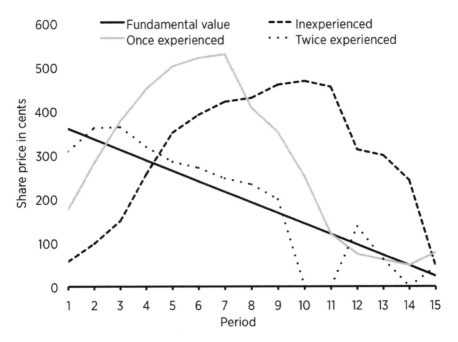

Source: Hussam et al. (2008).

# Bubble echoes in the wild

If we go back to real financial markets for a moment, we can try to identify these cynical bubbles. Figure 4.6 shows the drawdowns of the UK equity market since 1900. The bubbles can be identified by the significant crash that follows once each bubble bursts.

**Figure 4.6: Bubbles and bubble echoes in the UK stock market**

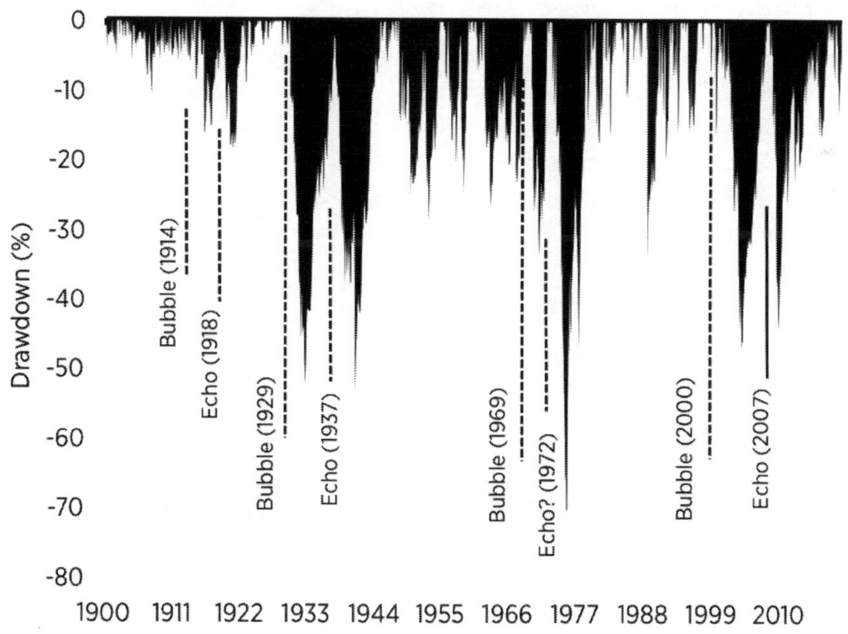

Source: Bloomberg, Bank of England.

What is striking is that these crashes seem to come in pairs, one bubble and crash episode being echoed by another bubble and crash episode a few years later. For example, the exuberance of the early years of the 20th century led to a market crash at the onset of the First World War in 1914. Once the war was over, investors expected the good times from before the war to continue, but when it became clear that the destruction of the war would limit growth and prosperity, stock markets declined yet again. The result was two significant crashes within four years.

The crash of 1929 triggered the Great Depression and ended the prosperity of the Roaring Twenties. However, during the early 1930s it seemed as if the worst of the depression was over and stock markets doubled, just to crash again by more than 50% in 1937, as it became clear that the depression was far from over.

Finally, the tech bubble of the late 1990s led to an almost 50% decline in the UK stock market between 2000 and 2002 as the bubble burst. However, the recovery after the recession of 2001 and 2002 was unusual in the sense that unemployment remained stubbornly high, and inflation did not pick up as much as it had in previous cycles. As a result, central banks left interest rates too low for too long and inadvertently fuelled a housing bubble that eventually collapsed in 2007, triggering the Global Financial Crisis of 2008.

In the UK stock market, there seem to be very few major stock market declines that were not followed by an echo in the form of another crash a few years later. The only major exception seems to be the crash of technology and growth stocks at the end of the so-called 'Go Go Years' in 1969. After their collapse, these growth and technology stocks recovered quickly, but their recovery was cut short by another significant market decline in 1972. However, this is not a true bubble echo, since the decline was triggered by an external shock, when OPEC refused to export oil to Western countries.

Overall, it seems as if investors have to experience two market bubbles and crashes in short succession before they learn to avoid them.

# Forgetting past experiences: rekindling a bubble

A cursory glance at the history of financial markets shows clearly that we had more than two bubbles and crashes in history. In fact, after a bubble echo bursts, there often is a longer period of relatively calm and well-behaved markets before another bubble forms and a new crash is in the making. Thus, it seems that while we learn from our experience for a while, at some point the lessons of the past are forgotten and new bubbles can form.

To investigate how this can happen, we have to return to the laboratory one last time and look at a final set of experiments. This time, the researchers let volunteers participate in the experiment a couple of times so that they could gather enough experience to avoid bubbles and cynical bubbles. Then they threw a wrench in the works of the experiment, by manipulating it in three different ways.

In one experiment, they gave each participant a lot more cash but the same number of stocks. This simulates an environment in which the central bank fights a stock market crash by lowering interest rates dramatically (or engaging in quantitative easing), increasing the supply of money significantly. The result is that more liquidity chases the same number of assets as before.

In a second experiment, the researchers left the amount of cash and shares alone, but significantly increased the potential variation in dividends. This simulates an environment where a new technology comes to the market that is as yet untested. Therefore, it has the potential to lead to significantly higher dividends and growth in the future, but also the risk of significantly lower dividends if the technology fails.

Finally, in the third manipulation, they mixed experienced with inexperienced volunteers and let them trade with each other. This simulates an environment where experienced investors retire and are replaced by younger, inexperienced investors.

The results in each of these three cases were similar. Figure 4.7 shows one typical result from these experiments. In each of the three cases, the researchers saw a new bubble form in the experimental market. The size of the bubble was similar to the size of the bubble seen with inexperienced investors, and the turnover amongst stocks was similar as well.

Figure 4.7: Rekindling a bubble with experienced investors

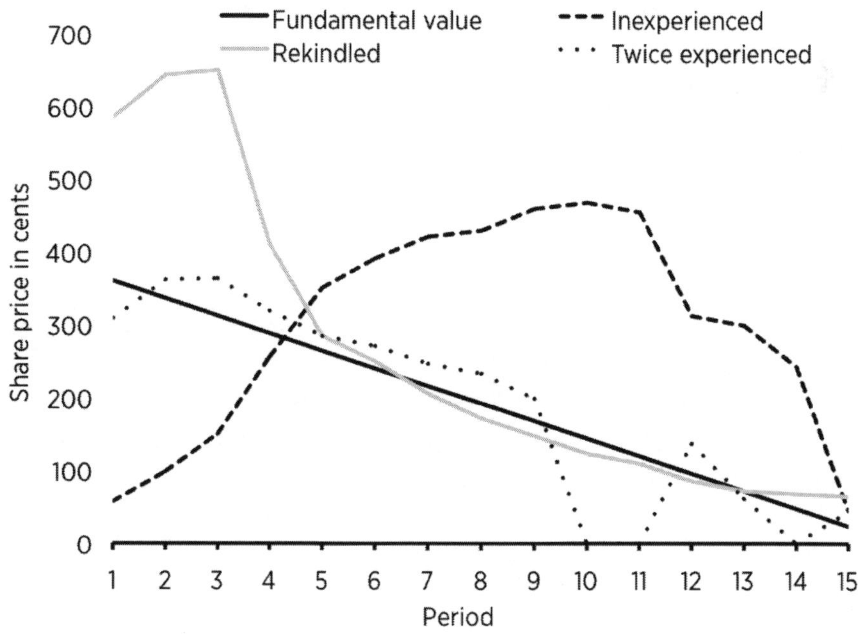

Source: Hussam et al. (2008).

However, the duration of these 'rekindled bubbles' was somewhat shorter than the bubbles observed in markets with inexperienced investors. This shows that the experience of past bubbles and crashes can be forgotten if some conditions are met.

New technologies and the euphoria about future growth in such technologies can create a new bubble, even if the market is full of rational and experienced investors. Central banks printing too much money, or providing too much liquidity in an effort to stimulate the economy, sow the seeds of a new bubble in the future. Lack of experience in young investors also makes markets vulnerable to fresh bubbles.

In fact, the researchers found that if inexperienced investors make up just one third of the total investor base, then bubbles can form again. If we assume that the average career of an investor is 30 years, then 10 years after a recession, about one third of investors have left the market and been replaced by new investors. If there was no recession or crisis during these ten years, as has been the case for example in the decade after the global financial crisis of 2008, then there is a sufficiently large minority of inexperienced investors in the market to rekindle a new bubble. Together with the massive liquidity expansion by central banks in the decade after the global financial crisis, and the advent of new technologies like social media and artificial intelligence, this provides fertile ground for the next great bubble to form.

# Career risk as an obstacle to learning from experience

The laboratory experiments described in this chapter, and others like them, can explain why bubbles and crashes form in financial markets time and again, and probably will continue to do so for eternity. But they do not explain why investors take such a long time to learn from the past, and why so little is learned from history. Ironically, it seems as if the institutional practices of the investment industry can provide a formidable obstacle to learning from past experiences.

I have written in Chapter 2 about the detrimental effects of short-termism on the performance of fund managers and individual investors. But this focus on the short-term also prevents some fund managers and other investors from learning from the past. Take a study by Gary Porter and Jack Trifts in 2012, which set out to identify the qualities of fund managers that have had an exceptionally long and successful career.

They started with a set of 41,248 funds run by 15,225 managers. In order to find out the role experience plays in fund manager performance over time, they selected only those funds that were managed by a single fund manager (as opposed to a team of managers), and where a fund manager was in charge of the fund for at least ten years. How exceptional these cases are can be seen by the number of funds in their original set that met these criteria: 355 (less than 1% of the original number of funds). These 355 funds were run by 288 fund managers, ranging from celebrities such as Peter Lynch of Fidelity and Bill Miller of Legg Mason, as well as lesser known managers.

One of the key findings of the study was that fund managers do not have time to learn from past mistakes, and improve their performance, if they had a bad start. Solo fund managers, whose tenure lasted just three years or less, had an average underperformance relative to the market of 1.33% per year before their funds were shut down. The fund managers that lasted ten years or more, on the other hand, had an average outperformance relative to the market during the first three years of 1.18% per year.

Thus, even if you are a talented manager, if you underperform during the first three years, your investors and your employers will abandon you and you will be forced to shut down your fund. If, on the other hand, you have a strong performance during the first three years of your tenure, you are allowed to continue. The bias of investors and investment companies to look at the short-term performance of three years, eliminates some managers that may have generated great performance over longer time frames.

## Most fund managers get worse with experience

This tendency also has another unintended consequence. If you were successful with whatever you did in the first three years of your tenure, you tend to keep doing the same thing in the future. After all, if you change your investment approach and start to underperform, your investors have a reason to abandon your fund and your employer has a reason to replace you with another fund manager.

So, even though markets change, the investment processes of fund managers remain remarkably inflexible to change. The result is that a fund manager's performance tends to decline over time since they re-apply processes that worked in the past, even though they don't work anymore.

Figure 4.8 shows the first three years' performance of fund managers with a more than ten-year track record, as well as their performance in subsequent years. The study of Porter and Trifts didn't just look at all the fund managers who started with a strong average outperformance of 1.18% per year in the first three years, and then declined to a rather small outperformance of 0.5% per year in subsequent years. It also separated the fund managers that had top quartile performance in the first three years, and the ten best managers in their sample.

**Figure 4.8: Performance of fund managers with experience**

The top quartile managers saw their outperformance decline from 6.8% per year, in the first three years, to 4.6% per year afterwards. It was only a select few managers at the very top of the list that managed to replicate their original success of the first three years. Since it is almost impossible to identify these true investment stars before they become stars, this means that investors, on average, have to face an inconvenient truth: the funds they select, and the managers they invest in, will likely have worse and worse performance the longer they manage their funds.

Consider this the next time a fund management company, or a fund manager, uses the years of experience a manager and his team have to advertise a fund. The implicit claim is that more experience makes them better investors yet, in practice, it likely makes them worse.

# Individual investors don't learn from the past either

But it's not just professional fund managers that fall into the trap of repeating what has worked in the past and then seeing their performance decline over time. Individual investors make the same mistake. In 2018, a study by William Bazley and his colleagues tracked 1,499 individual investors who opened a new account with a US brokerage firm throughout the first three years of their trading activity. Figure 4.9 shows their average monthly performance over time.

**Figure 4.9: Investment performance of retail investors**

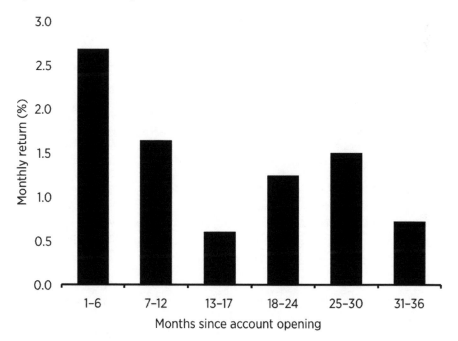

Source: Bazley et al. (2018).

The study found that the performance of these individual investors declined dramatically over the first six to 12 months. The reason for this decline in performance was that investors tended to be influenced significantly by the experiences of their first few trades after opening an account, as well as their most recent trades.

This effort to do what had worked in the past, and avoid what had not, led to a decline in performance of roughly 3.2% per month. That the decline in monthly performance measured in the experiment (and shown in Figure 4.9) is just 2.1%, and thus smaller than 3.2%, has to do with the fact that investors are not completely immune to learning from experience and did improve some aspects of their portfolio.

Over time, investors learned to diversify their portfolios more and reduce their trading activity. These effects counteracted the decline in performance somewhat, but the net result was still a significant reduction in performance over time.

# Learning from experience

The experiences we have as investors can be used as powerful tools to improve our investing. All we need to do is start learning the right lessons and, gradually, we get better and better at investing. This does not mean that we will achieve perfection and become the next Warren Buffett or Peter Lynch. Most of us are mere mortals and do not have the extremely high level of skill shown by these investment legends.

Thus, no matter how much we learn from experience, we should expect to continue to make investments that will lose money, either because we made a mistake in our process or in our investment rationale. This is all a part of investing and, at least for me, part of what makes it fun.

Markets are constantly changing. As I will show in Chapter 7 of this book, this makes it impossible to predict them or find an investment approach that works all the time. But, if we are able to learn from past experiences, we hopefully won't make the same mistake twice (or three or four times). And that alone dramatically reduces the number of mistakes in our portfolio.

Funnily enough, in order to systematically learn from past experiences and improve our investment performance, we do not need fancy investment tools or even a high level of investment knowledge. All we need is pen and paper, and the ability to be honest with ourselves. I am going to show you how an investment diary and an investment checklist can have a significant impact on your investing.

## Your investment diary

One of the most important components of my investment process is keeping a diary – in fact, it's the tool I have used for the longest time. The idea of an investment diary is simple. For every investment decision you make, you write down what the decision is, why you think the investment should work and make a profit, and what the risks are to the investment (why it could go wrong).

You don't have to write an entire novel. Just three short bullet points explaining your decision and reasoning are enough. You also don't have to embarrass yourself by showing the diary to anyone. Like a regular diary, it contains some of your most private thoughts and, thus, should be kept to yourself or only shown to people you trust.

As an example, take a look at the investment diary entry in Figure 4.10. In summer 2019, I bought a tactical (short-term) position in US stocks, in an effort to benefit from the potential boost stock markets may get if the US central bank cuts interest rates for the first time in many years.

**Figure 4.10: A sample investment diary entry**

---

**19 June 2019**

- Invested $10,000 in S&P 500 ETF with an investment horizon of three to six months.

- Why: Federal Reserve is expected to cut interest rates in summer in order to boost a slowing economy. This should give US stock markets temporary support but won't be enough to avoid a recession further down the road.

- Risk: Rate cuts by the Fed could already be fully priced in or markets could interpret rate cuts as a signal that a recession is imminent, leading to a decline in US stocks.

---

When I wrote this entry there were many unknowns about the investment. Historically, US stock markets have rallied briefly when the US central bank cuts interest rates for the first time in a while. This is because the cut in interest rates means that businesses and private households can get cheaper loans and mortgages. This may incentivise them to take out a loan, or increase their mortgage to make investments, or buy more expensive consumer goods like a new car.

Historically, the first rate cut of the central bank comes at a time when the economy is not yet in a recession, but when it slows down from past levels of strong growth or when inflation is well below the target the central bank tries to maintain. In this environment, growth fears are not yet strong enough to create a widespread fear of a recession, which would obviously be very bad for stocks. Instead, at the time of a first rate cut, investors tend to be neutral to slightly optimistic on the economic outlook and hope that the rate cut will spur inflation, in turn pushing stock prices higher.

The risks to this investment are manifold. While, historically, buying stocks when the central bank cuts interest rates for the first time has worked on average, it has not worked every time. In some cases, like 2007, the central bank cut interest rates so late that the recession was already underway. As a result, the rate cuts came at a time when more and more investors realised that the economy was in decline, and that future corporate profits would decline significantly and possibly even become negative. Thus, the rate cut of the central bank failed to boost equities, and equity prices declined rapidly. Similarly, stock markets may have already anticipated a rate cut so, when the rate cut is announced, stocks will do nothing.

As I write these lines, I do not know what the result of this investment decision will be, but once I sell the ETF again, I will make another entry into my investment diary that states when I have sold the ETF, what the outcome (in terms of performance) was and whether I was right or wrong in my reasoning.

Here, honesty becomes an important part of the process. Often, an investment makes a profit for different reasons than we anticipated. Or, we may have anticipated some risks, but other unexpected events led to a negative outcome. Part of the investment diary entry should be to note down if you were right for the right reasons, or if you just got lucky.

We humans have an incredible ability to justify our actions after the fact. For example, stock markets may continue to rise because economic data from the US is improving, and investors become more optimistic about the outlook for future corporate profits – not because of the interest rate cuts by the central bank.

If we don't write down our original reasons for our investment decision, we often fall into the trap of thinking that we saw the improvement in economic outlook coming and that this is why we made the investment in the first place. If you write an investment diary that contains the reasons why you made the investment, you have a much harder time convincing yourself that you knew it all along.

In this respect, I also recommend writing your investment diary by hand. If you see your decisions written down in your own handwriting instead of typed letters, it becomes much harder to convince yourself that you didn't mean what you wrote in the past, or to blame your mistakes on someone else (e.g. your financial adviser or the expert on TV). Part of the process is to be honest with yourself and take responsibility for both your successes and your failures.

## Review your diary at least once a year

Finally, you need to do more than just keep an investment diary. Once a year, I sit down and go through all my entries of the last year and systematically review my investment decisions. I do this to find patterns of behaviour that have led me to make mistakes.

A warning: this will not boost your self-confidence! Looking at your investment diary entries will make you realise how often you were wrong, and how often you were just plain lucky (i.e. right, but for the wrong reason). It is truly a humbling experience. On the other hand, this is exactly the point in time when you learn from past mistakes and have a chance to become a better investor.

Over the years, I have learned many things about my own investment decisions. One of the first things I learned from reviewing my investment diary was that I was much better at selling than buying.

My career as an investor started during the technology bubble of the late 1990s and one of my first investment decisions was to buy a fund that invested in technology stocks. At first, the fund performed extremely well, as technology stocks were in a bubble. But once the bubble burst, I held on to the investment for too long and eventually sold it with a steep loss.

If that sounds familiar, it is because I acted precisely like the young fund managers in the study of Greenwood and Nagel, discussed at the beginning of this chapter. I was a believer in the bubble, and I got severely burned. In the aftermath, I saw bubbles everywhere. I wanted to avoid the losses I experienced previously at all costs, so I tended to sell investments at the first sign of trouble. This had the practical advantage that I sold some of my stocks before the financial crisis hit in 2008. I did not predict the financial crisis ahead of time, and I did not sell all of my stocks but, because of my extreme fear of losses, I sold some positions in late 2007 and got lucky because markets tanked afterwards.

However, this fear of loss also prevented me from buying into stock markets at the early stages of recovery. Stock markets tend to look several months into the future, so when the economy is still in bad shape, and the news is uniformly bad, that is often the best time to invest in stocks. This is because if the news gets only a little better in the future, share prices will rise. As the old adage goes: buy when blood is running in the streets.

Looking through my investment diary for the years 2008 and 2009, I quickly realised that I bought stocks far too late in 2009, when a lot of the recovery was already over. Furthermore, the amount of money I invested in the recovery was lower than the amount I sold before the crisis. In the end, I did only a little better than a buy-and-hold investor during the financial crisis. I could have done much better if I had been able to overcome my doubts and invest sooner.

As a result of this analysis, I decided to make some changes to my investment checklist. I decided to introduce a mechanical rule that would override my emotions in the early stages of a market recovery. I simply added a point to my investment checklist that said I would have to invest the same amount I previously sold, once a stock market index climbed above its 200-day moving average, or rallied by a certain percentage from its three-month low (see Chapter 3). No matter what I thought the risks were, I forced myself to follow this rule and my performance has improved significantly since then, simply because I don't miss out on recoveries anymore.

## Your investment checklist

"Wait," I hear you say, "What is that investment checklist you mentioned in the last paragraph?" Investment checklists are the second tool in my toolbox for learning from experience. There are a lot of factors that can influence an investment and, over time, the things you learn about yourself and financial markets can become so manifold that it is impossible to remember them all. We have a limited capacity to remember things and we often have to work in a complex environment. No matter how much of an expert you are, there are things you will forget to do from time to time.

Atul Gawande, in his wonderful book, *The Checklist Manifesto,* tells the story of how the introduction of checklists for pilots of aircraft led to a dramatic decline in crashes, and how the introduction of checklists in an operation room reduced the number of patient deaths significantly. Value investor extraordinaire, Guy Spier, adapted this idea to investment processes. Because he is a stock picker, his checklist is ostensibly geared towards checking all the details of a company's balance sheet, cash flow statement, its profitability and management, etc.

In his book, *The Education of a Value Investor,* Spier describes how his checklist contains some very exotic questions like, is the company's CEO going through a divorce or some other life crisis? I presume he learned from experience that such events can distract a corporate leader to such a degree that the profitability of the company might be in danger.

In my case, my investment checklist is geared towards my own investment style, which is more oriented towards macroeconomic trends and developments. I hardly ever buy single stocks in my portfolio, but rather invest in diversified funds (index funds as well as actively managed funds). Because of the lessons I learned from my investment diary, my checklist is mostly concerned with taking my emotions and biases out of the investment process, and introducing mechanical rules where needed.

What matters, though, is not the exact details of my checklist or any other person's checklist. Just like an investment diary, they are very personal and cannot be copied from some other person. Rather, you need to develop an individual checklist by following a constant process of making investment decisions, writing them down in a diary, reviewing the diary, incorporating the learnings from the diary into an investment checklist, and then using that checklist the next time you make an investment decision.

This way, you create a constant feedback loop that allows you to learn from your experiences, in a highly individual way, and has a good chance of improving your performance over time (Figure 4.11).

**Figure 4.11: An investment process that learns from experience**

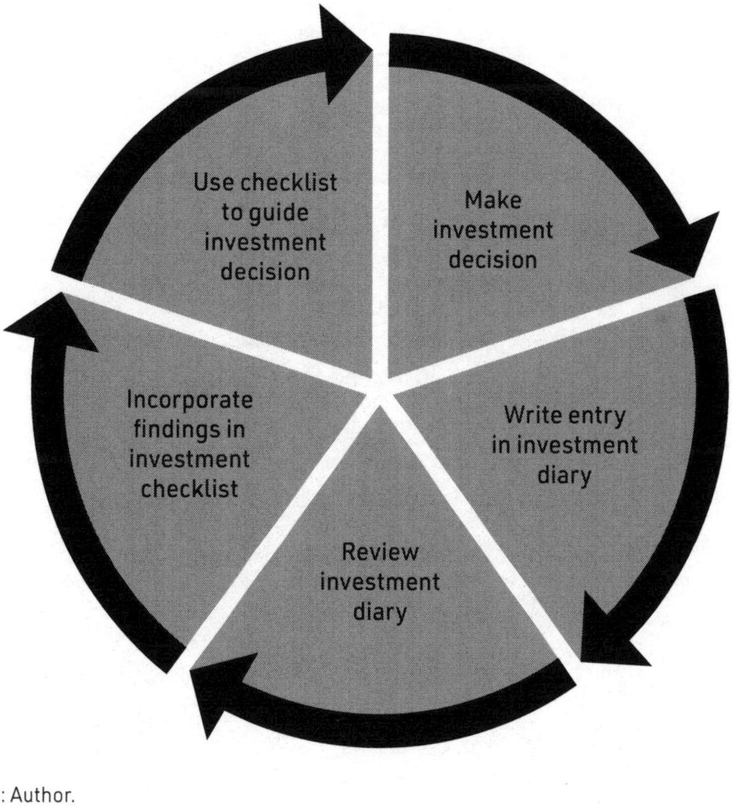

Use checklist to guide investment decision

Make investment decision

Write entry in investment diary

Review investment diary

Incorporate findings in investment checklist

Source: Author.

# Main points

- The investment decisions we make are influenced by our experiences as investors. Younger, less experienced investors invest differently and in different assets than older investors.

- Unfortunately, there is little evidence that our investment performance improves as we get more experienced. Our experiences change our investments, but they typically do not improve them.

- Laboratory experiments show that investors learn about markets and learn to avoid bubbles and crashes if they experience them often enough. However, learning happens slowly, and investors typically have to go through several boom and bust cycles before they learn to recognise them.

- This slow learning can lead to bubble echoes, i.e. circumstances where two major market bubbles and crashes follow each in other short intervals before market participants finally learn their lesson and start to behave more rationally.

- Unfortunately, we tend to forget lessons from the past and younger, less experienced investors may never have learned the lessons to begin with. Thus, after some time, history starts to repeat itself to some degree.

- In order to speed up the learning process, and avoid making the same mistake twice, I recommend keeping an investment diary that contains each investment decision, the reason why it was made and the risks to the investment.

- At regular intervals, the investment diary should be honestly reviewed to identify systematic biases an investor has. To avoid the negative impact of these biases, investors should commit to specific investment rules.

- These rules should form an investment checklist to be followed before each new investment. This way, new investment decisions actively reflect learnings from past experience.

# References

W. J. Bazley, G. M. Korniotis and G. R. Samanez-Larkin, "Why memory hinders investor learning", ssrn.com/abstract=2846504 (SSRN, 2018).

Y.-M. Chiang, D. Hirshleifer, Y. Qian and A. E. Sheerman, "Do investors learn from experience? Evidence from frequent IPO investors", *The Review of Financial Studies*, v.24 (5), p.1560–1589 (2011).

J. Deese and R. A. Kaufman, "Serial effects in recall of unorganized and sequentially organized verbal material", *Journal of Experimental Psychology*, v.54 (3), p.180–187 (1957).

R. N. Hussam, D. Porter and V. L. Smith, "Thar she blows: Can bubbles be rekindled with experienced subjects?", *American Economic Review*, v.98 (3), p.924–937 (2008).

A. Gawande, *The Checklist Manifesto* (Metropolitan Books, 2009).

R. Greenwood and S. Nagel, "Inexperienced investors and bubbles", *Journal of Financial Economics*, v.93 (2), p.239–258 (2009).

G. Nicolosi, L. Peng and N. Zhu, "Do individual investors learn from their trading experience?", *Journal of Financial Markets*, v.12 (2), p.317–336 (2009).

D. P. Porter and V. L. Smith, "Stock market bubbles in the laboratory", *The Journal of Behavioral Finance*, v.4 (1), p.7–20 (2003).

G. E. Porter and J. W. Trifts, "The best mutual fund managers: Testing the impact of experience using a survivorship-bias free dataset", *Journal of Applied Finance*, v.1, p.1–13 (2012).

G. Spier, *The Education of a Value Investor*, (Palgrave Macmillan, 2014).

# CHAPTER 5

## IGNORING THE OTHER SIDE OF A STORY

et's go back in time to the year 1998. US stock markets are gripped by what eventually would be known as the technology bubble of the late 1990s. The opportunities of the newly developed internet seem endless, and information technology seems bound to revolutionise our world.

To benefit from these innovations, a computer is needed, but, in 1998, only about one third of US households have one. This will change rapidly. Only two years later, more than half of US households have a computer and, by 2015, this will rise to nine out of ten (Figure 5.1).

You want to benefit from this trend, but how? One way would be to buy shares of manufacturers of hardware, like IBM, or of computer chips, like Intel. But you are a smart investor (after all, you have perfect foresight about the future spread of computers), so you notice that the market for computers, processors and other hardware is competitive, with many companies constantly trying to undermine each other in terms of pricing. This, you understand, will diminish their profit margins and eventually reduce their profit growth. But not all is lost.

**Figure 5.1: Prevalence of smoking and computers in the US**

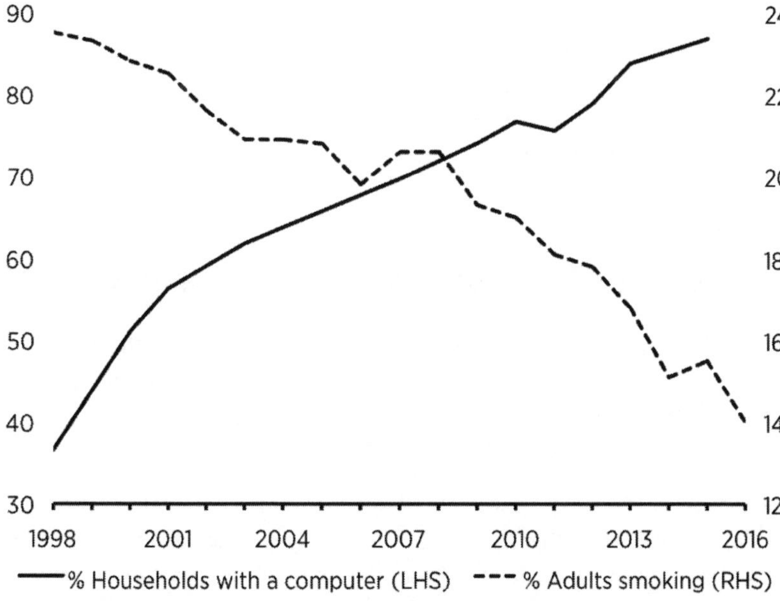

% Households with a computer (LHS)    - - - % Adults smoking (RHS)

Source: CDC, US Census Bureau.

There is one company that has a quasi-monopoly on a crucial part of this technology. Microsoft's Windows operating system is installed on virtually every computer in the world. In the late 1990s, about 98% of computers worldwide are running on Windows software (in 2019, this market share is still 87%).

Every economic textbook in the world states that while monopolies are not good for consumers, they are great for investors, because monopolies dictate the price of their product and thus have pricing power. As a result, profit margins should remain high and, given the likely future growth in the number of computers installed in households, you would expect profits to grow rapidly. Microsoft shares look set for a golden future.

The fast growth in information technology is in stark contrast to the fate of the tobacco industry. For decades, big tobacco has claimed that smoking was not hazardous to your health, even in the face of mounting evidence that smoking causes cancer and other diseases. By the mid-1990s, several states in the US are suing tobacco companies, claiming that the companies knew about the health risks of their products, creating massive costs to state-run health plans like Medicare and Medicaid.

Faced with this multitude of lawsuits, the major tobacco companies – Philip Morris, R. J. Reynolds, Brown & Williamson, and Lorillard – enter into a settlement with the state attorneys of 46 states that forced them to pay $206bn over 25 years. Furthermore, the companies are banned from advertising to young persons and have to contribute billions to efforts aimed at reducing youth smoking.

The effect on tobacco consumption will be dramatic (Figure 5.1 shows that, between 1998 and 2015, the percentage of adult smokers in the US declined from 23.5% to 15.5%). Saddled with these massive costs, and the decline in demand for their products, big tobacco seems to be doomed and it is surely only a matter of time until their shares are close to worthless.

## The outcomes for investors were vastly different

If you had told anyone in 1998 that you would buy shares of Philip Morris (later to be renamed Altria), and sell your shares in Microsoft, people would have doubted your mental health given the megatrends described above. Yet, as Figure 5.2 shows, this is exactly what a long-term investor should have done in 1998.

At first, Microsoft shares outperformed Altria shares by a wide margin, as the technology bubble continued and investors in big tobacco digested the costs of the settlement. Shares of Altria fell 18% in the first half of 1998, as the terms of the settlement became known to investors, while Microsoft shares rallied 40% over the same time. The outperformance of Microsoft would continue until the tech bubble burst in the first few months of the year 2000.

From then on, however, it was a one-way street, with Altria shares generating a return of 17% per year between 2000 and the end of 2015, and Microsoft shares stagnating with a return of essentially zero. It was only with the technology boom since 2015 that Microsoft could catch up and eventually overtake Altria.

**Figure 5.2: Share prices of Microsoft and Altria**

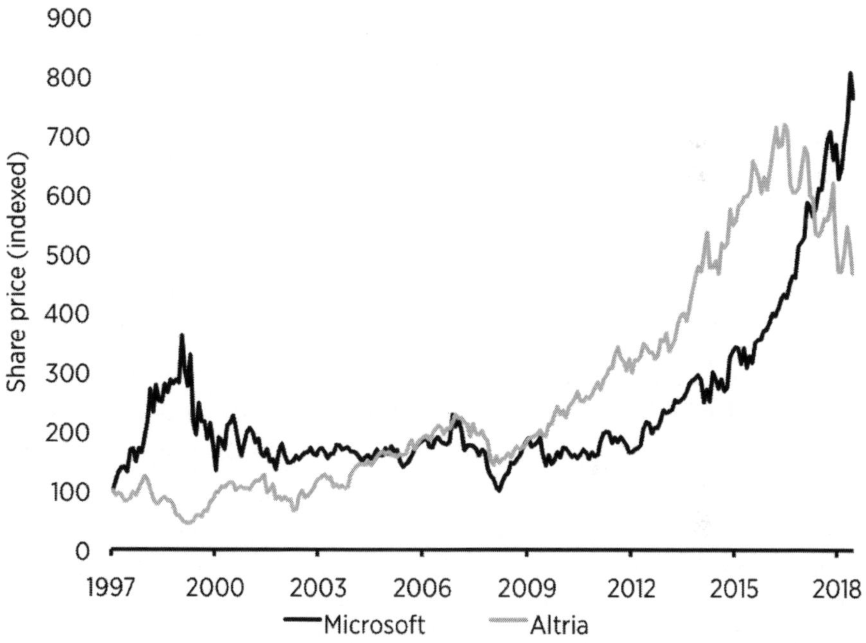

Source: Bloomberg.

How is it possible that the share prices of Microsoft and Altria behaved so differently from the underlying trends shown in Figure 5.1? How could the shares of a company that was on its way to bankruptcy (Altria) outperform the shares of a company that had a monopoly on a crucial growth technology for almost 20 years?

# A crucial mistake

The crucial mistake made in Figure 5.1, and unfortunately it is one of the most common mistakes made by investors all over the world, is to look at only one side of the story. One of the fundamental tenets of economics is that prices are the result of supply and demand, but Figure 5.1 shows only the demand side. The demand for computers by American households (and households all around the globe, for that matter) rose steadily, and with it the demand for the Windows operating system produced by Microsoft. But what about the supply?

In the 1990s, young entrepreneurs started a whole host of new technology companies that would gradually transform the world. For example, a young guy named Jeff Bezos started a company called Amazon to sell books over the internet. In May 1997, Amazon went public and, today, it is one of the largest companies in the world, making Bezos the world's richest man.

Venture capitalists were eager to finance many of these young entrepreneurs and help them develop their ideas. The result was the launch of Google and the rise of social media like Facebook. The development of IT also led to new hardware technologies, like smartphones, a trend that Microsoft missed for a long time.

If all electronic devices are counted instead of just PCs, as I have done above, then the market share of Microsoft Windows today is just 38%, on par with Google's Android at 37%. Apple's iOS and OS X operating systems together have a market share of 21%.

Thus, what used to be a quasi-monopoly for Microsoft in the late 1990s, has become a three-way race 20 years later. And with this increased competition from new suppliers came a decline in profit margins and a lack of growth that bedevilled Microsoft and its share price for more than a decade.

But while the supply of operating software and IT solutions has rapidly increased since the late 1990s, the supply of tobacco products has decreased significantly.

Go back to the list of tobacco companies that entered into the settlement agreement in 1998. Philip Morris still exists and was renamed Altria, after it spun off its international operation into a separate entity called Philip Morris International in 2008. R. J. Reynolds merged in 2004 with Brown & Williamson, the American operations of British American Tobacco, and renamed itself Reynolds American. In 2015, Reynolds American bought Lorillard, and the combined company was in turn bought by British American Tobacco in 2017.

After 20 years, what used to be four big tobacco companies competing for market share has turned into two. In a sense, supply, or at least the competitive pressure in the tobacco industry, has declined. The result was that tobacco companies could recover from the settlement and expand their profit margins to such an extent that it more than compensated for the decline in demand from smokers.

This kind of mistake is all too common with investors. When it comes to assessing supply and demand, forecasting demand tends to be easier and makes for a better story that investors can relate to. In 2008, oil prices rose above $100 per barrel for the first time. The main driver of this move was strong demand from China which, at the time, was the second largest consumer of oil after the US. China was projected to grow its oil demand rapidly in the coming years and, indeed, between 2008 and 2018, the monthly oil imports of China rose from 15m to 40m barrels.

Back in 2008, these projections led to fears about peak oil, i.e. the risk that we would run out of oil soon and face ever-rising prices as supply could not keep up with demand. Instead, supply expanded massively because the high oil prices made new technologies (such as fracking) profitable and led to a massive expansion of US oil production.

The result was a steep decline in oil prices to below $30 per barrel in 2016. This, in turn, led to worries about an oil glut, as investors projected the supply growth at the time into the future, and became afraid that China and the US would be unable to cover the vast supply of shale oil and gas. But, at these low prices, many producers of shale oil were no longer profitable and had to curtail production, or even went into bankruptcy, which in turn reduced supply, etc. (Figure 5.3).

**Figure 5.3: Price of crude oil**

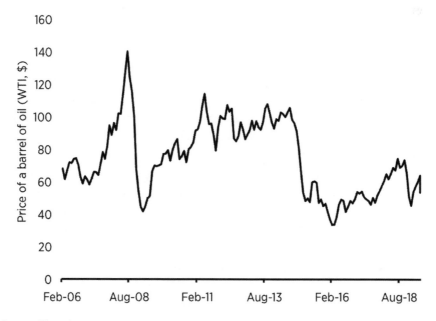

Source: Bloomberg.

In this chapter, I will focus on the impact that neglecting the other side of the story has on investment portfolios. As we will see, looking only at growth of demand, while ignoring supply (or vice versa), is an all too common human trait. We are constantly looking for confirmation of our beliefs, and have a hard time dealing with information that contradicts our views.

Counteracting these natural impulses is hard in practice but, at the end of the chapter, I will try to show how a disciplined effort to change how you digest information can help.

## We don't like to be contradicted

Ever since the US presidential election in 2016 and the UK Brexit referendum in the same year, there has been an intense discussion about echo chambers – the tendency to listen only to news that confirms one's political viewpoint. The increasing polarisation of the media is exemplified by cable news networks, like Fox News and MSNBC, over the last two decades in the US. But most of the blame is put on social media, such as Facebook, which presents news to users based on algorithms that identify which content engages them most.

To see if these echo chambers really exist, Walter Quattrociocchi and his colleagues at Harvard University set up two experiments, one amongst 279,000 Italian Facebook users, and another amongst 9.8m US users. The researchers analysed the likes and posts of the users from 2010 to 2014 to separate users into scientifically minded users, who would share factual information and reports that focus on recent research findings in different fields, and conspiracy-minded users, who would read, comment and like posts that promoted conspiracy theories.

The researchers then confronted these Facebook users with two different kinds of posts. In Italy, the researchers created what is commonly known as a troll factory, i.e., Facebook sites that post sarcastic and paradoxical content mocking conspiracy theories. In the US, the researchers launched Facebook sites that debunked conspiracy theories with the help of data and information.

Then they measured how often the conspiracy-minded users would engage with the different content. The results are striking and shown in Figure 5.4. Of the conspiracy minded users in Italy, about 15% interacted (e.g. liked or commented) with the intentionally false information. No matter how outlandish the troll factory claims may have been, a large minority of the conspiracy-minded users were willing to accept the claims and help distribute them across Facebook.

**Figure 5.4: Interactions with information on Facebook**

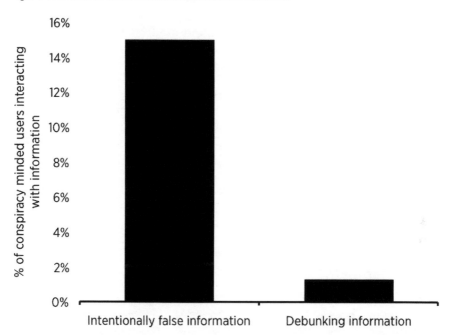

Source: Quattrociocchi et al. (2016).

If confronted with information intended to debunk conspiracy theories, however, conspiracy-minded users were much less likely to engage. Less than 1.3% of conspiracy-minded users liked or commented on the debunking posts placed in the US. When confronted with information contradicting our pre-existing beliefs, we tend to ignore it as much as we can.

## Test your confirmation bias

To discount information that contradicts our beliefs and seek out information that confirms them is known as confirmation bias, which has long been documented by psychologists. A classic example is a study by Charles Lord, Lee Ross, and Mark Lepper from 1979.

They recruited 151 students who held opposing views on the death penalty and provided them with two randomly selected texts, out of a pool of 20, on the death penalty. Some texts argued in favour of the death penalty, while others argued against it. The result of this exercise was not a consensus between the participants but, instead, an increased polarisation of the participants.

People who were in favour of the death penalty discounted the texts arguing against it and instead became more convinced that the death penalty was a good deterrent against crime. People who were against the death penalty became even more ardent opponents, as they discounted the texts that argued in favour of it as a deterrent to crime.

We all tend to think of ourselves as objective people who are able to weigh arguments for and against a topic but, in reality, we are likely to be much more biased in our ability to look for contradictory information than we realise. In 1971, Paul Wason and Diana Shapiro designed a simple experiment to show this bias. You can try it yourself:

Imagine you are an administrator at a university, and you must check if report cards are marked correctly. The cards have a letter on one side and a number on the flip side. The rule that must be checked is if the card has the letter D on one side, it must have the number 3 on the flip side. Figure 5.5 shows four report cards that you need to check.

**Figure 5.5: Which cards to turn over?**

Source: Wason and Shapiro (1971).

Obviously, the easiest way to check them would be to turn over all four cards and check them manually. But that is a lot of work since you have many more cards to check than just these four. Thus, the task for you is to check the minimum number of cards to make sure the rule is not violated. Which cards do you have to turn over?

Figure 5.6 shows the percentage of people that chose different cards to turn over in the original experiment. About half the people confronted with the task chose to turn over the cards marked D and 3. Turning over the card marked D directly checks if the flip side has the number 3 on it, while the idea behind flipping over the card with the number 3 is to check if it has a D on it.

But remember the rule stated above. It only says if there is a D on one side the other side must have a 3, not the other way around. By turning over the card with the number 3, the participants are looking for confirmation of their prior belief that the flip side says D.

In fact, the correct cards to turn over are the ones marked D and 7. If you turn over the card with the number 7, and it shows the letter D, you have found a contradiction to the rule. But as Figure 5.6 shows, only one in 25 people turn over just the cards with the letter D and the number 7.

**Figure 5.6: Answers to the selection task**

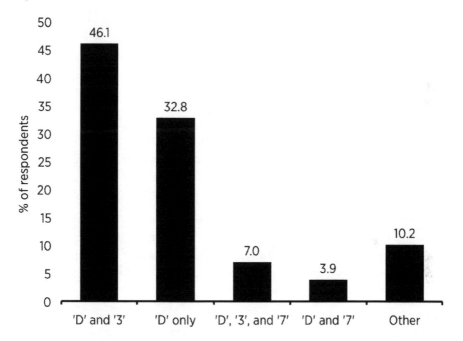

Source: Wason and Shapiro (1971).

If you still don't understand why turning over the cards D and 7 is the correct answer, let me restate the experiment in terms that are less abstract. Assume you are a bartender and you have to make sure that no underage person drinks alcohol. The rule you must check is that if someone is under the age of 18 (D), this person may only drink non-alcoholic beverages (3).

As you look around your bar, you see four people. One person is 16 years old (D), the second person is 30 years old (K). The third person drinks a non-alcoholic beverage (3) and the fourth person drinks beer (7). Which people do you have to check? In this case, most people will immediately check if the 16-year old drinks an alcoholic beverage (turning over card D) and check the age of the person who drinks beer (turning over card 7).

Don't feel bad if you did not get the right solution in the abstract selection task above. When I did it for the first time, I turned over the cards with the letter D and the number 3 like most people. It just goes to show that most people have a hard time looking for information that contradicts their beliefs, and that we need to actively engage to counteract this confirmation bias.

Because it is easy to search for information that confirms our view, and discount information that contradicts it, investors make mistakes like the ones discussed at the beginning of this chapter where they look only at the demand for computers and cigarettes but not at the supply. Importantly, this behaviour, in my view, gives rise to the allure of growth.

# The allure of growth

Growth is one of the cornerstones of many investments. Consequently, many investors are constantly on the lookout for things that can be invested in and which grow over time. The fundamental value of a company is driven by the present value of future corporate profits, and the faster these profits grow in the future, the higher the value of a company.

Industries that promise particularly high growth rates in the future thus attract a lot of attention amongst investors, and the valuation of companies that operate in these industries tend to be much higher than the valuation of companies in other industries. Of course, these higher valuations are justified if future growth turns out to be as high as investors expect today.

But here we encounter the problem we saw with Microsoft at the beginning of this chapter. Investors typically only look at growth in demand for a company's products and services, tending to ignore the competitive forces at play that influence supply. We have seen in Chapter 1 that even experts are horrible at forecasting, even if these forecasts are for short horizons such as one year. And their forecasting error increases as the investment horizon expands.

For companies operating in high-growth industries, such as IT, or that produce new goods and services that are largely untested in the marketplace, the forecasts must be accurate many years and decades into the future to get an accurate measure of the value of the company.

As long as a high-growth company can meet or exceed market expectations for future growth, its share price will soar. This has been the case, over the last decade or so, for the FAANG stocks (Facebook, Apple, Amazon, Netflix, Google), which have achieved extremely high growth rates and, as a result, have become some of the most valuable companies in the world.

Over the last decade, the average earnings growth rate of Amazon has been 30% per year, compared to 11.6% for the S&P 500 index of US stocks. If Amazon can defend these stunning growth rates, the shares of the company will continue to be a great investment.

However, analysts estimate that the long-term average growth rate of Amazon's earnings will be 45% per year, even higher than the company managed to achieve over the last decade, and about five times as high as the estimated long-term growth rate for the S&P 500.

Despite analyst forecasts being typically very unreliable, let us assume that the estimates for Amazon are the best guess investors have for the future growth of the company. I am a fan of Amazon as a business, but basic arithmetic says that growth rates must decline as the company becomes bigger. If a company has earnings of $1m per year and increases those earnings to $2m per year, that is a growth of 100%. But if a company has earnings of $2m per year and then increases them by $1m per year, that is a growth rate of 50%. Assuming that Amazon will be able to grow its earnings at 45% per year over the next several years requires an enormous amount of optimism about the market opportunities available to the company. And it assumes that there will be no competitor able to take market share from Amazon in the future. History shows that both assumptions are highly unrealistic.

Thus, it is pretty safe to say that Amazon will not be able to grow its earnings by 45% per year forever. Whether it is in a year or ten years, at some point investors will have to adjust their growth expectations downward. And when that happens, the share price of Amazon will decline rapidly, since lower expected earnings growth implies a dramatically lower valuation for the company overall.

The tech bubble burst of 2000–2003 shows how far technology stocks can drop if investors have overly optimistic assumptions about future growth that are not met. The Nasdaq Composite Index of technology and other growth stocks in the US dropped 75% between February 2000 and September 2002.

# The safety of value

Contrast this behaviour of growth stocks with the situation for value stocks. Value stocks offer comparatively cheap valuations. These cheap valuations can be the result of different factors, but most often reflect a lack of growth prospects or that a company or industry is in distress and it is unclear if and how it can survive. Thus, investors effectively price low or sometimes negative growth into the valuation of these companies.

Some of these companies will not be able to survive and eventually end up in bankruptcy. But the vast majority of companies will continue to operate, and the growth prospects will improve, at which point investors will adjust their expectations upwards and the share price of these companies will rise. The example of Altria, at the beginning of this chapter, shows how investors who just look at growth prospects may miss the potential changes in supply that can lead to higher profit margins and higher growth in the future.

The outperformance of value stocks versus growth stocks is well-documented and can be demonstrated in almost all stock markets in the world. Figure 5.7 shows the results of a study by Eugene Fama and Ken French for 13 stock markets between 1975 and 1995. With the exception of Italy, value stocks outperformed growth stocks by at least two percentage points per year.

**Figure 5.7: Outperformance of value versus growth**

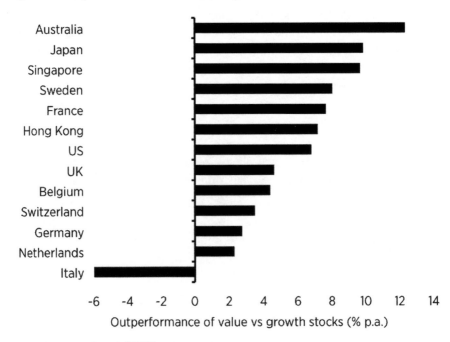

Outperformance of value vs growth stocks (% p.a.)

Source: Fama and French (1998).

If value stocks outperform growth stocks by 2% per year for 20 years, a basket of value stocks is worth 1.5 times the value of a basket of growth stocks at the end. In the case of Australia, where the outperformance was more than 12% per year, the basket of value stocks is worth nine times more than the basket of growth stocks after two decades. Investors who are too enamoured by growth thus leave a lot of money on the table.

# Economic growth and stock returns

Another example of investors being overly focused on growth, and ignoring evidence that contradicts their beliefs, is the link between economic growth and stock market returns. I don't know how often I have seen some salesperson or fund manager argue that we should invest in China or India, because these economies have much higher growth rates than the Western world.

The argument is typically that higher economic growth leads to faster sales growth for companies operating in this market, which in turn should translate into higher earnings growth. The unspoken assumption about this argument is that companies operating in these high-growth countries can keep their profit margins at current levels.

But if an economy grows at a very fast rate, it will attract investments from all over the world. Unless a country is closed to foreign investors, these new entrants will compete with existing companies in the market, and this increased competition will drive profit margins down. Thus, while sales grow fast, the decline in profit margins may lead to low or even negative growth rates for companies in these countries.

Just like Microsoft lost market share to new entrants in the technology space, domestic companies in fast-growing economies lose market share to new entrants from abroad and at home. Figure 5.8 shows the relationship between economic growth (measured as real GDP per capita growth) and the real return of stock markets in the country's home currency.

**Figure 5.8: Economic growth and stock returns in 19 countries**

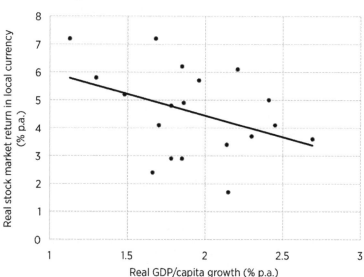

Source: Ritter (2012).

The data shows that, on average, higher economic growth leads to lower stock market returns, not higher stock market returns. The study shown in this chart is based on large-cap companies in 19 developed economies around the world. I have reproduced the same study with 22 developed and 22 emerging economies, as well as using both large and small-cap companies. None of the cases showed a positive relationship between economic growth and stock market returns.

## Engage with views you disagree with

The best investors in the world have the remarkable ability to engage with views and beliefs that contradict their own, and incorporate them into their investment process. For instance, Peter Lynch, the legendary fund manager of the Magellan Fund, was a growth investor. But he knew that with the allure of growth came the risk of overpaying for future growth.

Thus, he pioneered the concept of Growth at a Reasonable Price (GARP). In this approach, Lynch combined elements of growth investing with elements of value investing, and his success at doing so speaks volumes. In the 13 years he managed the Magellan Fund, from 1977 to 1990, he outperformed the market by 12.8% per year.

This chapter has shown a few ways that investors interpret charts. Figure 5.9 shows the projected growth in electric vehicles worldwide. Most investors will look at this chart and say something along the lines of: "Wow, I have to invest in electric vehicles and battery technology to profit from this growth." And when they look at investment opportunities in the field, they may come across companies like Tesla, which dominates the market for luxury electric vehicles today.

**Figure 5.9: Projected electric vehicle sales**

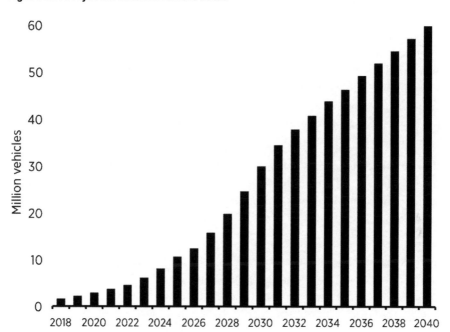

Source: Bloomberg, New Energy Finance.

But, after reading this chapter, you are more likely to consider not only the demand for electric vehicles, but also the supply. Is Tesla going to continue to dominate the market for luxury electric vehicles in the future, or are other companies – like the German luxury car makers – going to enter the market and reduce Tesla's profit margins? In 2018, Jaguar launched the I-Pace electric car. In 2019, while Audi launches the e-tron, Mercedes introduces its EQC electric car. All of these cars compete directly with Tesla.

If your reaction to Figure 5.9 was to question supply, then congratulations: you are now considering both sides of an investment story and are likely to improve your investment performance in the future.

But the examples given in this chapter are only the beginning. Challenging your beliefs is not easy and requires constant practice; like a muscle, it will get stronger as you exercise it. Your next goal should be to utilise your critical thinking. There are two important tools for doing this.

# Change your reading habits

Most investors get their information from a rather small number of sources. They may read a financial newspaper, like *The Wall Street Journal* or *Financial Times*, and complement this with occasional sessions watching investment-related shows on TV. The younger generation may get a lot of information via Twitter and podcasts, while more sophisticated investors have access to research from brokerage firms and asset management companies.

Yet, no matter your personal choice, the number of sources for investment information tends to be small – typically five or less. Often, the sources have similar opinions. All too often, I encounter investors (both private investors and investment professionals) who get their information from a monoculture of opinions.

Equity investors tend to fall into two camps: the eternal optimists, who can only see stock markets rise, and the permabears, who see the end of the world looming behind every corner. Even amongst professional investors, it is rare to find people who are able to transform their outlook as the data changes, yet those who can go from optimism to pessimism tend to be the most successful investors I know.

The problem is that investors who adapt their views based on the data are unlikely to become famous. It is often better for the career of a pundit to stick to one worldview for as long as possible – this makes for a great story and is what financial news likes to quote. If you constantly look at both sides of a story, you face being ridiculed.

US President Harry Truman once quipped: "Give me a one-handed economist. All my economists say, 'on the one hand…', then, 'but on the other'." While this frustration is understandable, it is also a mistake.

Compare your own habits of getting investment information with mine. (Admittedly, I am a professional investor though, so I can devote more time to investing than most people.)

On a regular (often daily) basis, I get an update on the most recent market developments on Bloomberg; I read research reports published by a wide range of asset managers on SavvyInvestor; I read several emails with abstracts of the newest academic research sent to me by SSRN, the IMF, the World Bank and the Bank for International Settlements; I read the free books and papers published by the CFA Institute Research Foundation, a not-for-profit organisation that I sit on the board of; I read the links to new investment insights collected by Tadas Viskanta at abnormalreturns.com; and I read 15 different free investment blogs whenever the authors publish a new article. On top of that, I follow journalists working at a range of economic newspapers on Twitter.

At the end of this chapter I have provided links to the free investment blogs I regularly follow. Some of them are famous and have a large following; others have a more select audience. You will find that the authors write from very different perspectives, ranging from chronically optimistic to chronically pessimistic. And, in many cases, I find their views… well, let's just say if I agreed with them, we'd both be wrong. But that is exactly why I read these papers, tweets and blog posts. If I agreed with most of what I read during the day, I would be doing something wrong.

I realise that the list of information sources I consult on a regular basis may be daunting for most non-professional investors: do not despair. As I mentioned above, when discussing the selection experiment with the four cards, at first, I failed the test miserably. Back then, I was reading just a few investment sources, like most people. When I learned about the trap of confirmation bias, I started to exercise my muscle of critical thinking more vigorously.

What you see in my list of resources, and what I have described in the previous paragraphs, is the result of 20 years or so of constant practice and fine-tuning of the information sources that I find useful. My intention is not to intimidate you, but to provide a head start on your journey.

## Your new best friend: the devil's advocate

Everybody needs a good friend to rely on when life gets tough. In investing, everyone should have a devil's advocate. The role of the devil's advocate is to challenge your investment beliefs by asking difficult and critical questions. Ideally, the devil's advocate will try to prove you and your investment ideas wrong.

For private investors, this might be a friend who does not have the same beliefs as you. For example, I am a big believer in sustainable investing and the integration of environmental, social and governance (ESG) criteria in the investment process to evaluate risks that are normally overlooked.

However, I have friends and colleagues who are convinced that ESG investing is just another hype that will lead to the next big bubble in financial markets. While I strongly disagree, discussing the topic with these people helps me to question my views and not get caught up in my personal optimism.

Similarly, professional investors often manage their investment process as a team. The benefit of this approach is to involve a range of voices and viewpoints in investment decisions. The risk, however, is that groupthink creeps in, everybody starts to think alike, and nobody gets seriously challenged on their views.

In order to fight groupthink, some investment teams create the role of devil's advocate, whose job it is to challenge the other team members on their views – particularly when they all seem to agree. This approach can best be summarised by a quote from the movie *World War Z*, where a virus creates a global zombie apocalypse. The only country that manages to be prepared for this disaster is Israel. When the hero of the movie, played by Brad Pitt, asks the person who secured Jerusalem against the disaster how they knew to do so, the answer is: "If nine of us with the same information arrived at the exact same conclusion, it's the duty of the tenth man to disagree. No matter how improbable it may seem, the tenth man has to start thinking with the assumption that the other nine were wrong."

Investing is very different from the zombie apocalypse (at least most of the time), but the tool for preventing disaster is the same. A word to the wise, though. If a team assigns a devil's advocate, they should make sure to rotate the role from time to time. Otherwise, the person who has to play devil's advocate all the time will become very unpopular very quickly.

Besides, assigning the role of devil's advocate to the same person every time increases the chance of another form of groupthink, when all the team members automatically discount the arguments of the devil's advocate as invalid, simply because this person always argues against every idea.

## Main points

- Too often, investors fall prey to an alluring growth story without investigating the other side of it. If demand is projected to grow strongly, you should investigate how supply will react to that, and vice versa.

- Confirmation bias, our tendency to look for information that confirms our pre-existing views, and discount information that contradicts it, is a major obstacle to an impartial assessment of an investment opportunity. Confirmation bias leads to us living in echo chambers of like-minded people.

- Confirmation bias also gives rise to overly optimistic valuations for growth stocks, and overly pessimistic assessments of value stocks. This, in turn, can explain the outperformance of value stocks in the long run.

- The best way to reduce confirmation bias, and get a more comprehensive picture of an investment, is to expand your information sources and systematically include information from sources that have opposing views of the same event or market.

- Another tool for fighting confirmation bias is to appoint a devil's advocate who will try to find holes in an investment idea.

# Free investment blogs

This is my personal diet of investment blogs. It is deliberately broad in views and content, and does not constitute an endorsement of any of these authors or sites. This list is by no means exhaustive; there are many good content providers out there.

## Curated content

CFA Institute Enterprising Investor, blogs.cfainstitute.org/investor

Tadas Viskanta, Abnormal Returns, abnormalreturns.com

## Individual bloggers writing on a wide range of topics

Michael Batnick, The Irrelevant Investor, theirrelevantinvestor.com

Josh Brown, The Reformed Broker, thereformedbroker.com

Ben Carlson, A Wealth of Common Sense, awealthofcommonsense.com

Joachim Klement, Klement on Investing, klementoninvesting.substack.com

Larry Siegel, larrysiegel.org

Jason Voss, Active Investment Management, www.jasonapollovoss.com/web/category/the-blog

## Quant stuff

Alpha Architect, alphaarchitect.com/blog

AQR Asset Management, www.aqr.com/Insights

Aswath Damodaran, Musings on the Market, aswathdamodaran.blogspot.com

Corey Hoffstein, Flirting with Models, blog.thinknewfound.com/blog

Jesse Livermore, Philosophical Economics, www.philosophicaleconomics.com

Research Affiliates, www.researchaffiliates.com/en_us/insights/publications.insights.html

## The "pessimists"

Jesse Felder, The Felder Report, thefelderreport.com

Phil Grant, (Almost) Daily Grant's, www.grantspub.com/resources/commentary.cfm

John Hussman, www.hussmanfunds.com/content/comment

# References

E. F. Fama and K. R. French, "Value versus growth: The international evidence", *The Journal of Finance*, v.53 (6), p.1975–1999 (1998).

J. Klement, "What's growth got to do with it? Equity returns and economic growth", *The Journal of Investing*, v.24 (2), p.74–78 (2015).

C. G. Lord, L. Ross and M. R. Lepper, "Biased Assimilation and Attitude Polarization: The Effects of Prior Theories on Subsequently Considered Evidence", *Journal of Personality and Social Psychology*, v.37 (11), p.2089–2109 (1979).

W. Quattrociocchi, A. Scala and C. R. Sunstein, "Echo chambers on Facebook", *Harvard John M. Olin Discussion Paper No. 877* (2016).

J. R. Ritter, "Is economic growth good for investors?", *Journal of Applied Corporate Finance*, v.24 (3), p.8–18 (2012).

P. C. Wason and D. Shapiro, "Natural and contrived experience in a reasoning problem", *Quarterly Journal of Experimental Psychology*, v.23, p.63–71 (1971).

# CHAPTER 6

## YOU GET WHAT YOU PAY FOR

So far, I have focused on the mistakes that investors – both professional and private – make in their investment processes, and how to avoid or overcome these mistakes. But let's face it: none of us has the skills or the time to cover all the different markets and investments available to us.

Even professional money managers must specialise in one area, such as European or emerging market stocks, to at least have a fighting chance of creating better performance than a market index. In the more esoteric spaces of alternative investments, the degree of specialisation needs to be even higher.

A couple of years ago, when I joined a small company specialising in alternative investments, I had the best part of two decades of experience as a professional investor. I could easily go on TV, or a panel of investment experts, and discuss the merits of the Swiss property market or the latest earnings report of Facebook. But the company I joined was active in alternative investments, ranging from structured finance investments to private equity deals in fintech.

Suddenly, I had to learn everything I could about the intricacies of collateralised loan obligations, and how covenants for the underlying loans have developed over time. And that is just one example. In time, I became proficient in the risks and opportunities of a whole new investment universe which was, at once, both extremely fascinating and complex.

But no matter how long I have been working in this field, I would never dare to start my own fund specialising in any of these arcane corners of the global financial markets. I am an investment generalist and, thus, I do not believe I can create superior performance in these areas.

If I want to invest in some highly specialised area, I must rely on the expertise of the specialists that I trust with my money. From the smallest retail investor to the biggest endowments and pension funds, managing a well-diversified portfolio always requires finding a balance between the things that you do yourself and the things that need to be outsourced. Typically, this outsourcing of investments happens in the form of fund investments and, in the institutional investment space, in the form of segregated managed accounts.

Trusting someone with your money requires this person to be trustworthy. Thus, the first task of an investor is to find money managers that aren't crooks. Sounds easy enough, but the long history of crooks that have managed to steal large amounts of money from unsuspecting investors – ranging from Charles Ponzi to

Bernard Madoff – continues to this day. But this is a book on investments, not criminology, so I leave the subject of how to spot a crook to people who know more about this than I do.

Instead, this chapter will focus on how to spot a money manager that can be trusted with your investments because they deliver value for money.

In well-established investments with a liquid market like stocks or bonds, the basic choice for an investor comes down to either paying extremely low fees for a fund that replicates a given market index, or paying higher fees for a money manager and their team in the hope of generating returns that surpass the index. For the former, getting value for money often means getting the index tracker with the lowest fees; in the latter, value for money comes down to looking for outperformance over index returns to be larger than the surplus fees charged by the money manager.

In alternative investments, and in illiquid investments like private equity, there are no index funds available that replicate a benchmark representative of the overall market. Value for money is often much harder to define in these spaces, as it requires an assessment of the money manager's ability to generate returns that are attractive relative to the risks of the investment, or that create diversification benefits in a portfolio.

But, as you might have guessed, this is another area where many investors make mistakes that are detrimental to their wealth. In this chapter, I will review what, in my view, are the most common mistakes investors make when selecting external money managers, and I'll provide tips on how to identify managers that do provide value for money.

While I will focus mainly on the selection of mutual funds, based on the insights researchers have gained on equity mutual funds, the mistakes presented here, as well as the tips to improve performance, are generally applicable to alternative investments as well. So, don't write me a complaint letter if I focus predominantly on equity funds in this chapter; it is merely a shorthand for active money management in general.

## Active fees for passive funds

Most investors know that, after fees, the majority of actively managed funds underperform their benchmark index. Figure 6.1 shows the share of funds investing in European, US and emerging market equities that manage to outperform their benchmark after fees over a rolling 12-month horizon.

**Figure 6.1: Share of funds outperforming their benchmark after fees**

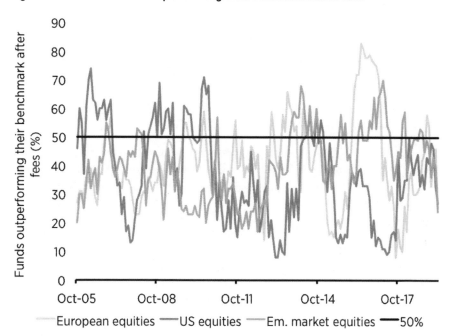

European equities ━━US equities ━━Em. market equities ━━50%

Source: Bloomberg.

On average, only about two in five funds outperform their benchmark after fees in any given 12-month period. And because only very few funds manage to consistently outperform their benchmark every year, the percentage of funds that outperform over three, five or ten years very quickly declines towards zero.

The challenge is, of course, to identify the few funds that can provide good value for money (i.e. outperformance over the benchmark after fees) before they do so. As we have seen in Chapter 2, investors often make the mistake of assuming that past performance is an indication of future outcome and invest in those funds that have outperformed their benchmarks during the last couple of years.

This can destroy performance if the period used to evaluate past performance is too short. In those cases, investors become victims of short-termism in their investment decisions. But if past performance is not a good criterion to select money managers, what is?

It may sound obvious, but the first step for an investor should be to select funds that have a reasonable chance of outperforming their benchmark to begin with. Unfortunately, this is where the mistakes start. In 2016, the European Securities and Markets Authority (ESMA) analysed more than 2,600 funds registered in

Europe with at least €50m in assets under management and a management fee of at least 0.65% per year.

These funds charged fees that are typical of actively managed funds and were marketed as active funds. In order to test how active these funds really were, ESMA used three metrics. The first metric was the active share of the fund; that is, the percentage of the fund's portfolio that deviates from the index itself. For example, if company A has a weight in the index of 5%, but averages 8% in the fund, then the active share of that stock would be 8% − 5% = 3%.

The second metric investigated was tracking error, the degree of variation of a fund's performance around the performance of the index the fund tries to beat. Finally, ESMA looked at $R^2$, which is the percentage of variation in fund return that can be explained by the index itself.

In the narrowest case ESMA investigated, it would look at funds that had an active share of less than 50%, a tracking error of less than 3% and a $R^2$ of more than 95%. In other words, more than half the portfolio is identical to the index itself, the fund return fluctuates in a very narrow band around the index, and more than 95% of the fund performance could be explained by the index itself.

ESMA found that 5% of all funds they investigated fulfilled these criteria. These are funds that charge active fees, and pretend to be active, but even the most well-meaning observer could not describe them as anything else but an index fund in disguise.

If the criteria are relaxed only a little bit, to an active share of 60% or less, and a tracking error of 4% or less, then 15% of the so-called actively managed funds are caught. These are all candidates for closet indexing funds – charging active fees but managing their portfolios so close to their benchmark that they have virtually no chance of outperforming their benchmark after fees.

## Why are fund managers becoming less active?

It is only in recent years that active share has come to prominence as a measure of how actively managed a portfolio really is. Pure index funds typically have an active share of less than 20%, while a portfolio is typically considered actively managed if its active share is higher than 60%. Antti Petajisto and Martijn Cremers popularised this measure in 2009, I will discuss its use for investors later in this chapter.

What is interesting to note, however, is that in a study of US equity mutual funds in the early 1980s, Petajisto found that practically every fund was managed with an active share of 60% or higher. By 2009, the share of funds managed with an active share of 60% or more had dropped to half.

You have to wonder why the active share of mutual funds has halved since the 1980s? In my view, the driving force behind this rise of closet indexing behaviour amongst fund managers is career risk.

Put yourself into the shoes of a fund manager who manages a global equity portfolio for investors. In your role, you will try to attract investors to trust you with their money. But, before they do so, they will try to assess your ability to create value for their investors. A good way to do that is measure your alpha (i.e. outperformance over the benchmark index corrected for systematic risk) and beta (i.e. how risky the fund is relative to the benchmark index).

If you can show consistent and positive alpha over the long run, they will rain money on you like manna from heaven. But if you show negative alpha, they will take money away from you. As a fund manager, you can try to improve your chances of receiving the blessing of these people in several ways.

First, you can try to define a benchmark that is easy to beat. If you are an equity fund manager, you can claim that you want to achieve positive absolute returns over time (i.e. your benchmark is 0), or you may claim you want to achieve positive real returns after inflation (i.e. your benchmark is inflation). Unfortunately, investors aren't stupid, and they know that equities, on average, have positive returns that are significantly higher than inflation. So, they insist that you measure your equity fund against a meaningful benchmark, such as the MSCI World or FTSE World index.

Now we have an arms race on our hands. You, as the fund manager, grudgingly accept a market benchmark as your yardstick. But you know that if you tilt your portfolio towards small-cap and value stocks, you have a chance to outperform this benchmark in the long run, because small-cap and value stocks tend to have systematically higher returns.

At this point, you are essentially running a smart beta ETF, an index fund with a systematic tilt towards a risk factor that provides outperformance, such as value or momentum, under the label of an actively-managed fund. The active share of your portfolio is probably somewhere between 20% and 60% and the ESMA study would most likely classify you as a closet indexer.

Your investors are a really smart bunch; they can see that you are taking more and more systematic bets in small-cap and value stocks and accuse you of style drift. That is, you are slowly drifting away from your original investment philosophy outlined to investors when you launched the fund. If you continue to make these style bets without investor permission for long enough, they will start taking money away from you. So, you have to stop running hidden style bets after a while. One day, you meet your buddy, who works for a hedge fund, for a drink. He tells you that you could try to invest more in private assets. Private assets have the advantage of being illiquid so their prices don't fluctuate on a daily basis. On top, they provide alternative beta, that is systematic exposure to risk factors outside listed equity markets and linked to private equity investments, for example.

## A very public failure

If that all sounds too contrived for you, think about Neil Woodford, who was at the heart of the biggest fund management collapse in the UK in 2019. Woodford became a star fund manager in the 1990s, when he managed to run a successful large-cap equity fund for Invesco. In 2014, he left the firm and set up his own shop.

Having made his name with large-cap stocks, it was easy for him to collect several £bn in assets for his new funds within a few months. However, what many investors did not realise was that, over time, his investment style had begun to drift. Having made his name with large-cap stocks, he increasingly invested in small-cap stocks, and later in illiquid stocks that were not listed.

In 2019, more than 80% of his portfolio was invested in small-cap and private equity investments. Woodford's funds consistently underperformed the large-cap stock benchmarks he had set for himself, so investors increasingly withdrew their money. But because most of his assets were now in illiquid shares, which were more difficult to sell, his funds ran into difficulties.

In spring 2019, he was forced by the regulator to close his funds for redemptions and enter what amounts to an orderly wind-down. Neil Woodford had essentially gone down the road I just described, but investors had not noticed until it was too late. The end result was that Woodford's reputation was destroyed, and many investors are sitting on investments that they cannot sell.

## An alternative way to lose money for investors

Neil Woodford might not have ended up where he did, had he done what so many other fund managers do. That is, instead of succumbing to style drift, and the temptation of illiquid investments in a liquid fund, you try to create positive alpha in a straightforward way. Namely, by fulfilling your promise to investors to pick stocks that outperform the market.

You are confident enough to believe that you can do this, but you are also aware that you have a family at home that is used to a certain lifestyle. So, you must earn an income to buy food and pay the mortgage. This means that you try not to lose your job.

You know that one way to lose your job is by underperforming your benchmark by too much or for too long, because your investors will withdraw their money from your fund. Now, it becomes tempting to change your investment process. In the past, you managed investment risk in your portfolio. This meant that you would try to avoid losses because investors pay you to make money, not lose money.

However, during the last bear market, you learned that investors did not write to thank you when your portfolio was down 15%, while the benchmark was down 20%. Similarly, during the recovery, when your portfolio was up 10% for three years while the benchmark was up 15%, none of them wanted their money back even despite your alpha being negative. What lesson does this teach you?

Instead of focusing on investment risk, you decide to focus on managing tracking error or active risk, i.e. the deviation from the benchmark index. This way, if you have a bad year, you won't underperform the benchmark by so much that your investors get nervous and start withdrawing money. Of course, by limiting the amount of active risk you take, you also limit the amount by which you can outperform the benchmark in a good year. But nobody is going to fire you just because you outperformed the benchmark by 2% instead of 5%.

## The impact of lower tracking error on investment performance

Figure 6.2 shows the effect this shift towards limiting tracking error has on your career risk. The chart shows the 95% confidence interval for out- and underperformance versus the benchmark, for a skilled manager who runs a fund with a 6% tracking error (solid line) and a fund with a 3% tracking error (dashed line).

By reducing the tracking error by half, the potential underperformance versus the benchmark is halved. Over a one-year horizon, the lower bound of the 95% confidence interval is raised from –8.8% to –4.4%. This can make the difference between keeping your job and being fired, since an underperformance of more than 5% in any given year would likely trigger a lot of fear in investors and your bosses. Thus, keeping it below psychologically important numbers, such as 5% or 10%, is important.

**Figure 6.2: The impact of tracking error on performance**

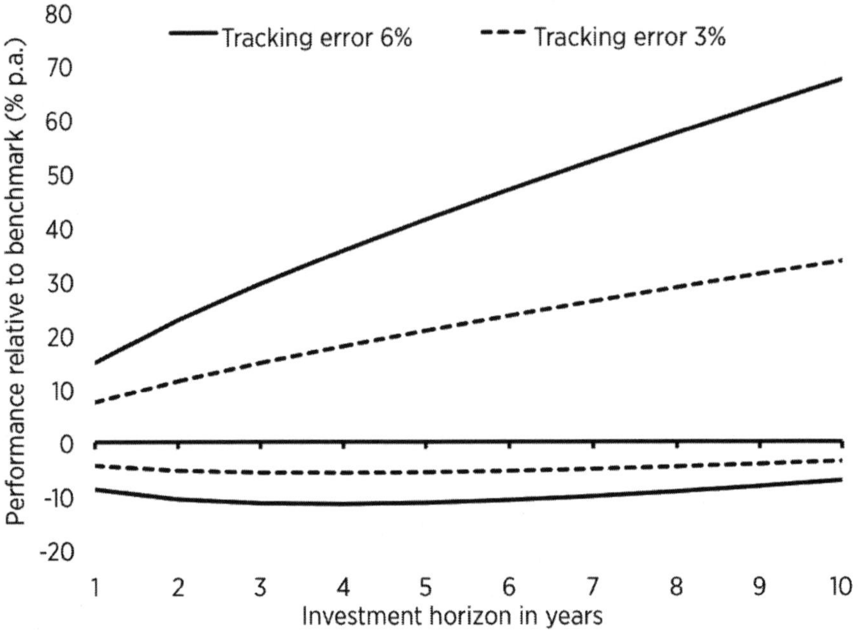

Source: Klement (2015).

Figure 6.2 also shows the cost to investors of your decision to limit tracking error. The potential outperformance over the benchmark is similarly halved. Over any given year, the upper limit of the 95% confidence interval is reduced from 14.8% outperformance to 8.4% outperformance, or, after ten years, from 66% outperformance to 33.6%. And these numbers are calculated before fees.

But, never mind the lost opportunity to add value to investors, this technique to limit your career risk works. If you have the skill to create positive alpha, your fund looks good on paper and creates outperformance over the benchmark index in most years. Your bosses are happy, because you are not losing assets, and you are happy, because you are getting a monthly pay cheque. The only ones getting screwed are your investors, because they get less performance than they could have, if you did your job with a higher degree of tracking error.

# Incentives matter

Astute readers will immediately ask how we can prove that such career risk considerations are at play when managing a fund portfolio. One way to test this is to look at the tracking error, or degree of activity, in funds with different kinds of ownership.

If a fund manager does not have a stake in the fund management company, but is solely an employee, then you might suspect that the incentive to reduce tracking error and active share becomes bigger. That's because the employee fund manager benefits less from the potential gains in fees from rising assets under management, but still risks being fired if the fund underperforms for too long.

In a company that is majority-owned by the fund manager or the employees, on the other hand, the incentive structure is much more symmetrical, with employees taking the risk of losing their job, but benefitting from rising assets under management.

With the help from colleagues at Fidante Partners and Alphinity Investment Management, I looked at the data of 1,471 global equity funds. When these funds are categorised by ownership, the average active share of funds managed by companies with 0% employee ownership is five percentage points lower than the active share of funds managed by companies that are majority employee owned.

Thus, while there is likely no conscious decision by fund managers to reduce the active share or tracking error in their funds, the incentive structure under which they operate pushes them in one direction or another.

But who cares about active share or tracking error, anyway? After all, what investors want from a fund manager is to achieve the best returns possible without taking undue risks. And reducing tracking error and active share at least reduces the risk of underperforming a given benchmark by a wide margin.

I will not go into the subject of whether investors should care about their performance relative to an arbitrary benchmark index (they should not). Instead, I shall focus on the fact that the job of an active manager is to identify attractive securities and use their creativity and expertise to generate high returns independent of the gyrations of a benchmark index.

That's what active managers are charging their fees for, and that is what they should be paid for. If an investor wants to achieve returns commensurate with an overall market index, they are clearly better off investing in an index fund or ETF.

# Employee-owned funds perform better

It seems that incentives, too, matter for performance. Figure 6.3 shows the performance of the global equity funds I have investigated before in relation to the ownership structure of the fund management company. The figure shows the average annual performance of the different groups of funds relative to the average fund performance.

It is immediately clear that fund companies that are majority owned by their employees run funds that have a better performance than companies that have no employee ownership. The difference between these two groups of companies is, on average, in the order of 0.5% to 0.7% per year. This is in the same order of magnitude as the fees charged by active funds per year!

Figure 6.3: Employee-owned firms do better

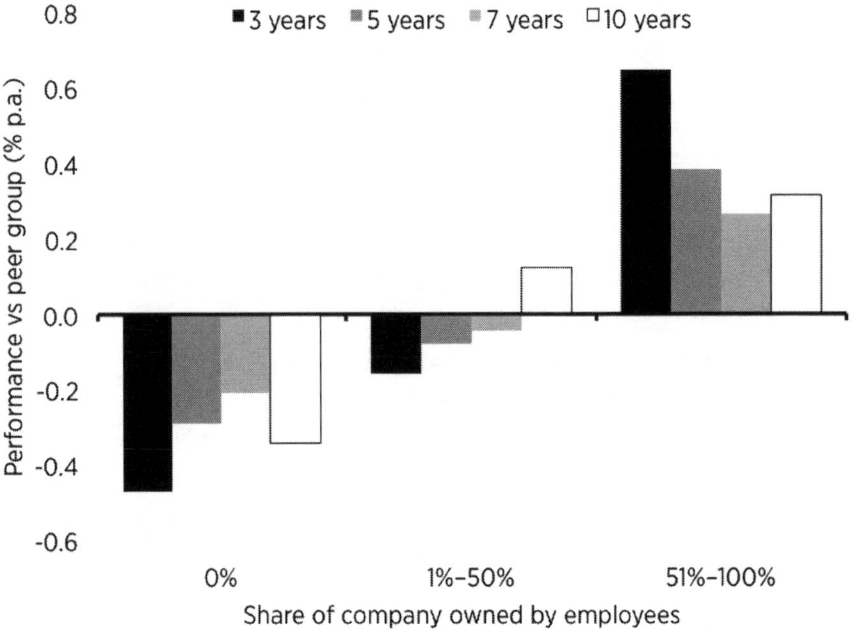

Source: Alphinity, Fidante Partners.

These results show that fund companies owned by fund managers and other employees tend to be more active and, as a result, have a better chance of outperforming their peers. There is, by now, a long list of research papers that have looked at the performance of funds where the manager is investing his or her own wealth.

In her doctoral thesis from 2008, Allison Evans looked at the amount of money fund managers had invested into their own funds. She found that fund managers who have more money invested in their own funds have higher returns both before, and after, taxes.

Funds with higher investments by their managers also tended to have lower turnover, creating lower management costs. Sadly, there was no relationship between the level of investment by the fund manager and the amount of investment inflows into the fund. In other words, funds with significant investments by the fund manager tended to perform better, but investors were not aware of this fact, and did not invest more money with these funds.

A paper published in 2019 by Linlin Ma and Yuehua Tang showed that this largely remained unchanged in the ten years since the research by Evans was published. Their paper found that the more money fund managers had invested in their funds, the better the performance was. It did not matter if fund ownership by the manager was measured in dollar amounts or in percentage of the fund's overall assets.

The more the manager had on the line, the better the performance was. Furthermore, this newer study found evidence that fund risk tended to decline if the fund manager had a larger stake in the fund, proving that once the fund manager has their own money at stake, they are less willing to make egregious bets or take on unnecessary risks.

What seems to have changed in the last decade, however, is that investors have become more and more aware of the positive effect that fund ownership has on the fund's performance. Unlike in the earlier study, Ma and Tang found a significantly positive effect of fund ownership by the fund manager on future inflows.

## So do smaller funds

There are clearly exceptions to the rule but, in my experience, the funds and companies with a larger ownership by the fund managers and employees tend to be the smaller ones. This makes sense, because the large asset management companies tend to be publicly listed, where the employees of the company are only able to hold a minority share in the business.

For some large fund management companies, this minority ownership tends to be close to zero, creating the misalignment of incentives that I discussed above. These large fund companies often argue that they have a distinct advantage over smaller boutique firms because of the vast resources they can employ to find investment ideas.

A small shop with five employees or less will not be able to cover a universe of several thousand global stocks as well as a large firm with hundreds of analysts. Also, large firms tend to have a global presence, which means that they have Chinese analysts who speak Mandarin and can analyse the financial statements of Chinese companies far better than an American analyst in the US ever could.

Large asset management firms also have more money to hire the most experienced and, presumably, best fund managers. A small boutique, on the other hand, is often run by a few experienced managers that are supported by younger, less experienced analysts – often simply because these young analysts are cheaper.

If you attend the marketing presentations of these large asset management firms, you are typically presented with a world map dotted with their office locations all over the globe and some impressive statistics. Firm A might brag that they have 172 analysts all around the globe, with the fund management team of 15 portfolio managers and analysts who have a combined 3,768 years of financial market experience.

At the beginning of my career, I used to be impressed by these statistics. Today, I just ignore them. First, if you have ten analysts and portfolio managers with ten years professional experience each, that does not turn into 100 years of combined experience! I would argue it's just ten years of experience in total, since every person working in the fund has had largely the same experiences over the last ten years.

If the last global recession is more than ten years in the past, that means that no one working in the fund has ever experienced a recession in their professional career. And that is something I would really worry about. Second, these large fund management companies never show any proof that their vast number of analysts around the globe leads to better performance in their funds. The reason why they don't do that is because, typically, it doesn't.

Figure 6.4 shows the performance of the same 1,471 global equity funds I have analysed above but, this time, I have sorted the performance of the funds by the number of analysts and portfolio managers in each fund. Remember that these funds cover global equities from large-caps to small-caps, and thus have a universe of several thousand stocks to choose from. A small firm with five portfolio managers or less should thus be at a significant disadvantage to a larger firm.

Instead, small boutique funds outperform their larger competitors by a wide margin. If we compare the average performance of funds with five portfolio managers or less with firms with more than 20 portfolio managers, then the average annual performance of the smaller funds is 1.1% to 1.3% higher per year. Given that the typical management fee of an actively managed equity fund is somewhere in the region of 0.5% to 1.5% per year, it is almost as if investing in smaller boutique funds is for free because the average outperformance is about the same as the average fee.

**Figure 6.4: The boutique advantage**

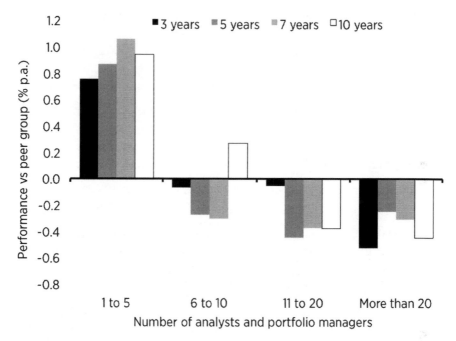

Source: Alphinity, Fidante Partners.

# A 1960s advertisement explains the advantage of smaller funds

There are many reasons why funds from smaller companies tend to do better than funds from larger companies. A better incentive structure is one of them, but nothing has ever expressed the advantages of a boutique asset management firm better than an ad for a car rental company.

In the early 1960s, the market for rental cars in the US was dominated by Hertz, with Avis being a distant second. The folks at Avis wanted to convince customers that they would get better service than at Hertz.

In many countries, ads cannot compare the product of one company to that of another in a biased way. Though you may be convinced that your product is better than that of your competitor, it does not go down well with customers if you tell them that the competition is rubbish. The market leader can always point out their principle position and let customers infer that this is because they have the best product. Why else would so many people buy their stuff? But the smaller competitor cannot do that. Should they say that their product is only second best?

In 2019, Danish brewing company Carlsberg relaunched its beer with a new recipe, explicitly stating that in the past they probably weren't making the best beer in the world. But such brutal honesty can only work if you have fundamentally changed your product. In the 1960s, such brutal honesty was unheard of and, besides, car rental, just like fund management, cannot reinvent its recipe.

So, Avis did something that nobody else had done up to that point. In 1962, they launched their "we try harder" campaign, which actively embraced their status as an underdog and succinctly stated why that lead to better service for their customers. Here is one of their ads, taken from *Ogilvy on Advertising*:

> "When you're only No. 2, you try harder. Or else.
>
> Little fish have to keep moving all of the time. The big ones never stop picking on them. Avis knows all about the problem of little fish. We're only number 2 in rent-a-cars. We'd be swallowed up if we did not try harder… And since we're not the big fish, you won't feel like a sardine when you come to our counter. We're not jammed with customers."

Boutique fund management firms can copy this advertisement today almost verbatim. Because of the wave of consolidation washing over the asset management industry in recent years, smaller fund managers are constantly at risk of being swallowed by the large asset managers with their manpower and capital.

In order to survive as independent businesses, they must try harder and be nimbler than those larger than them. And for customers, there is the additional benefit that they tend to be treated better by small fund managers, simply because they do not have as many customers. Thus, customers of smaller fund companies tend to have more access to the fund managers – the people running their money – than is the case in large firms.

Research shows that smaller funds, and smaller fund companies, have better performance than large firms across almost all asset classes. You might wonder what these large firms are doing all day, because the additional resources do not seem to turn into better investment performance.

Whenever you are at the marketing event of a large fund manager, you are experiencing first-hand what the additional resources of large firms are used for: attracting new investors. Leonard Kostovetsky and Alberto Manconi investigated more than 16,000 US-registered investment advisers from 2000 to 2016. They confirmed a couple of findings that have already been discussed in this chapter.

Firms with more employees ran portfolios with a lower active share and lower tracking error. They also had lower returns, though the variable that was more indicative of lower returns was the number of clients the firms had. As the number of clients increased, returns declined.

But there was one outcome that improved as the number of employees in a fund management company increased: assets. Bigger firms can afford a bigger sales force and can send their analysts and portfolio managers on marketing tours to convince investors to hand over their money. Instead of creating performance, the main activity of portfolio managers becomes asset gathering and marketing.

From the point of view of the company, that is exactly what they should do, since more assets invested in the firm's funds leads to more fee income, and thus more profits for the company. And, of course, bad performance would lead to outflows, so the important thing is to make sure that the performance of the funds can never be so bad as to create a mass exodus of clients. And this is easily done by reducing the active share and tracking error of the fund portfolios. We are back where we started. It's heads, the fund wins; tails, the investor loses.

This tendency of larger funds, and larger fund firms, to underperform is widespread across most asset classes, but I have to mention that there seems to be one notable exception. In the case of hedge funds, there seems to be an effect that larger hedge funds with more employees tend to have better performance than smaller funds.

Kostovetsky and Manconi also investigated hedge funds in their study, finding a positive relationship between the number of advisers in a hedge fund and its performance. Unlike mutual funds, hedge funds do not have to publicly disclose their performance. As a result, the hedge funds that disclose their performance, and that make up the constituents of prominent hedge fund indices, tend to be the ones that are open to new investors.

Large hedge funds that are closed to new investors, and have no intention of raising additional capital, tend to stop reporting their performance – even though these funds often have a very impressive long-term track record. This self-selection leads to a bias in reported hedge fund returns, where the largest hedge funds tend to have the best performance, but this is not publicly disclosed.

Daniel Edelman, William Fung and David Hsieh have shown that these mega hedge funds have distinct characteristics which set them apart from other hedge funds that report their performance. Lots of work still needs to be done to investigate this phenomenon, but it seems that large hedge fund firms are the exception that proves the rule laid out in this chapter. Unfortunately, because these mega hedge funds are, typically, closed to new investors, you cannot access this opportunity anyway.

# How to improve your investment performance

Picking funds that perform well is a hard task. Arguably, even harder than picking stocks. There are more than 80,000 mutual funds in the world, while the World Federation of Exchanges estimates the total number of publicly listed stocks to be around 50,000. Searching for funds that deliver value for money is like looking for the famous needle in a haystack.

There is no foolproof way to identify good fund managers and good funds. However, you can at least try to improve your chances by investing in funds that have a decent shot at providing value for money. In the case of actively managed funds, this boils down to avoiding funds that are closet indexers. Active share is a starting point, but by no means the endpoint.

Figure 6.5 shows the alpha generated by the US mutual funds used in the study of Antti Petajisto. It is clear that outperformance, in the long run, is concentrated in the funds with the highest active share. Just eliminating funds with a low active share increases your odds of selecting a good fund dramatically – something that has become clear to me since I first read their studies in 2013.

**Figure 6.5: More active fund managers deliver better performance**

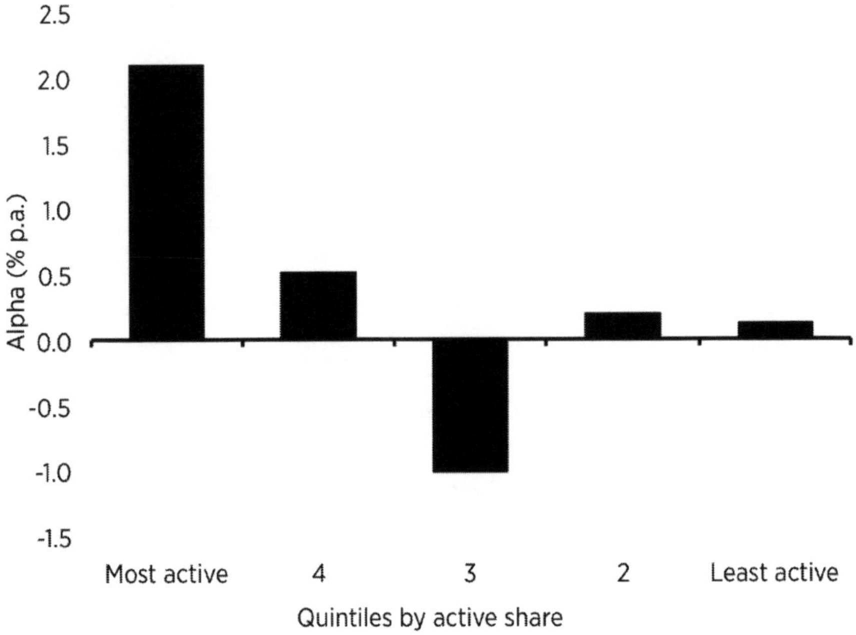

Source: Petajisto (2013).

Admittedly, I learned about active share a little bit late. Petajisto and Cremers first published their research on active share in 2009, but I only learned about it when Petajisto published an article written for investment professionals in the *Financial Analysts Journal* in 2013.

However, this timing was fortuitous, because an investor had just asked me to help him select a fund to cover US equities. The investor was not very happy with the performance of the fund he was currently invested in; it had lost him a lot of money during the financial crisis of 2008–2009 and had been slow to recover afterwards. In the end, after underperforming an index fund by a wide margin, the investor decided to change the fund in his portfolio.

Back then, I was working as an investment consultant in Switzerland and, having recently read the article on active share, I wanted to try it out. The list of funds to select from was initially very long, so we relied on the usual metrics, like past performance over a business cycle, risk relative to return, and consistency of returns, to narrow it down. But, even so, we were left with more than a dozen funds that all had a good track record, an investment process that made sense, and a range of awards to their name.

To simplify things, Figure 6.6 shows the performance of two of the best active funds in our sample, together with an ETF tracking the S&P 500. At the end of 2013, the younger of the two funds had been in existence since late 2007, so we chose to look at performance since the beginning of 2008 to give us an impression of how these funds fared during the financial crisis, as well as the recovery afterwards.

**Figure 6.6: Identifying good funds**

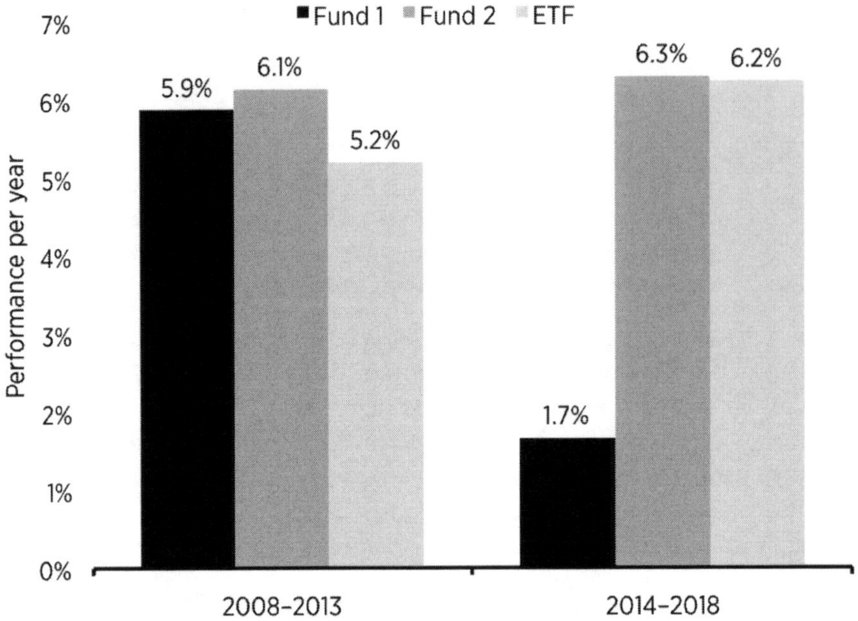

Source: Bloomberg.

As you can see, both funds did rather well and outperformed the ETF after fees. They also had similar risks and performed about the same during the financial crisis. Finally, traditional measures, like tracking error, were very similar. Fund 1 was from a renowned asset manager, with a broad range of funds and a global reach, while Fund 2 was from a medium-sized asset manager (though not a small boutique).

There was very little between the two funds, in terms of traditional metrics used to select funds, and most likely it would have come down to fees. This would have swung the decision in favour of Fund 1, which had an expense ratio of 0.69% per year compared to Fund 2's 0.8%.

But, being the nerd that I am, I decided to put the idea I had read about into action and calculated the active share of both funds. Lo and behold, Fund 1 had an active share of 38.5%, while Fund 2 had an active share of 74%. The manager of Fund 2 was really active, while the manager of Fund 1 hugged the benchmark index (in the case of both funds, and the ETF, this was the S&P 500). Because the fees of Fund 2 were not that much higher than the fees of Fund 1, we decided to invest in Fund 2, since the manager there had a better chance of outperforming the S&P 500 after fees.

Fast forward five years and Figure 6.6 shows how fortuitous this choice was. Over the subsequent five years, Fund 2 continued to outperform the ETF after fees, though by a very small amount, while Fund 1 significantly underperformed. Despite being a closet indexer, Fund 1 underperformed the index by a wide margin of 4.5% per year – something that is so unlikely in practice, that it surprises even me. Fund 1 has tried to reduce the chance of underperforming the index fund and still managed to deliver a disastrous performance, something that should give every investor pause. The underperformance of Fund 1 versus Fund 2 of 4.6% per year meant that every $100 invested in Fund 2 was worth $135.70 at the end of 2018, compared to $108.60 if we had invested in Fund 1.

## Active share isn't everything

This example highlights something else too, that a high active share does not always lead to outperformance of a fund with a low active share. A high active share means that the manager has a chance to add significant value, if the market allows them to. Markets do not always provide the same amount of opportunities for active managers.

In a stock market crash like 2008, investors tend to sell stocks independent of their individual merits. This indiscriminate selling means that even great stocks get sold off, and no amount of skill on behalf of the fund manager can create significant outperformance versus an index fund, or a closet index fund.

Similarly, in the fast recovery of 2009 to 2011, there was little dispersion amongst stocks; everything went up at the same time and by roughly the same amount. Again, not an environment where an active fund manager can add a lot of value.

What is needed for active managers to shine is an environment of high dispersion, where some stocks go up, some move sideways, and some decline. Anna von Reibnitz showed that the return difference between the most active and least active fund managers is negligible when dispersion amongst stocks is low or average.

Active share is only relevant in environments with high dispersion. For example, in periods of high dispersion, as we have seen in mid-2011, late 2015 and again in late 2018, funds with a high active share outperformed others by a wide margin. For investors, this means that it is impossible to predict when an active fund will outperform the market index, because periods of high dispersion are unpredictable and may last only a few months before subsiding again. It is the cumulative effect of many periods of high dispersion in markets that leads to the outperformance of highly active funds. In the end, investors need to stick with a highly active fund for an extended period of time to give the fund manager a chance to beat the market and benefit from the outperformance achieved over time.

# Small, active and employee owned

Today, I select funds differently than I did ten years ago. As I have stressed throughout this chapter, I am convinced that, in the fund world, you get what you pay for. If you pay for a big brand with glossy marketing brochures, you will get… a big brand that allows you to brag to your golf buddy about it. But, if you want a fund that has a good chance of outperforming the overall market, or a low-cost index fund, you should select different funds.

I have started to look for small boutique funds that are run by highly-active fund managers. These small funds are often ignored by banks and investment consultants, because they must focus on selecting large funds that they can recommend to a large number of clients. Thus, if you go to bank XYZ and ask for a fund recommendation, you will typically end up with the mega funds of the mega companies and, as we have seen in this chapter, these funds do not always have your best interests as an investor at heart.

Boutique funds cannot be recommended to the largest institutional investors, or a large number of private investors, because the money these investors would pour into the fund would overwhelm it. Furthermore, both banks and investment consultants run the risk of being fired by their customers if they recommend a small fund that no one ever heard of and it performs poorly.

"Nobody ever got fired for buying IBM," as they say. Buying a brand name provides protection against poor performance because "who could have known that these guys would screw up so badly?"

Fortunately, professional investors have an increasingly powerful set of tools at their disposal to identify these small, highly-active boutique funds. For example, professional databases, such as eVestment, provide a host of metrics on the funds in their database; information includes active shares, as well as the company and ownership structure of the fund.

This also allows professional investors to select funds that have the proper incentive structures for fund managers in place. Funds should be run by managers who have to eat their own cooking, meaning they should either be majority owners of their business, or have a substantial part of their personal wealth invested in their fund.

For retail investors, the task is arguably harder. Lacking access to professional databases means that they have to rely on public information from the different fund companies, or from service providers such as Morningstar. Unfortunately, fund providers do not have to disclose crucial metrics such as active share, nor the ownership structure of the fund management company.

Similarly, Morningstar and other public services do not provide this data on their websites, making it very difficult for retail investors to gain an advantage in their fund selection. There is an increasing number of websites and services for retail investors that try to publish this information, but the offering is so far very localised and not comprehensive.

Retail investors should not despair though, but rather keep Avis's "We try harder" ad in mind. As stated above, smaller firms have fewer customers, so their desks tend to provide a more personalised service. In this way, retail investors can test the service level of small fund management firms by simply picking up the phone and asking them to provide data on active share in their funds, and the incentive structure of the fund manager.

If the company responds quickly, and provides full transparency to you, the client, it is a sign of a company that will continue to provide good service once you have invested with them. If the company is evasive or ignores your requests because you are not a professional investor, then take your money elsewhere. If they don't need you, you don't need them either. Remember that there are more funds in the world than stocks.

# Main points

- Nobody is an expert in every corner of the financial market. We all have to delegate some of our investment decisions to outside managers.

- Finding managers that add value is very hard, since value means different things to different people. In most cases, selecting the index funds with the lowest costs should be the starting point for investors. Then, try to identify actively-managed funds that have a chance of outperforming their benchmark index.

- In order to have a better chance of finding managers that can outperform their benchmark, it is important to avoid funds that charge high fees for a low degree of activity. Active share is a good measure for identifying these closet index funds.

- Often, the incentives for a fund manager are such that it is better to become less active in the portfolio to avoid the risk of significantly underperforming a benchmark and losing clients.

- Besides a high active share, investors should look for funds from small, boutique companies with fund managers that have an incentive to create attractive returns. This typically means fund managers that have a large part of their personal wealth invested in their fund, and/or, that work for companies that are majority owned by their employees.

# References

Better Finance, "Better Finance replicates and discloses ESMA findings on closet indexing", betterfinance.eu (2017).

M. Butler, "City watchdog: We're taking action on asset managers that aren't transparent with clients", *The Telegraph* (5 March 2018).

K. J. M. Cremers and A. Petajisto, "How active is your fund manager? A new measure that predicts performance", *The Review of Financial Studies*, v.22 (9), p.3329–3365 (2009).

D. Edelman, W. Fung and D. A. Hsieh, "Exploring uncharted territories of the hedge fund industry: Empirical characteristics of mega hedge fund firms", *Journal of Financial Economics*, v.109 (3), p.734–758 (2013).

ESMA, "Statement on supervisory work on potential index tracking", *ESMA/2016/165* (2016).

A. L. Evans, "Portfolio manager ownership and mutual fund performance", *Financial Management*, v.37 (3), p.513–534 (2008).

J. Klement, "Career risk", *Journal of Behavioral Finance*, v.17 (4), p.336–341 (2016).

L. Kostovetsky and A. Manconi, "How much labor do you need to manage capital?", papers.ssrn.com/sol3/papers.cfm?abstract_id=2896355 (2018).

L. Ma and Y. Tang, "Portfolio manager ownership and mutual fund risk taking", *Management Science (forthcoming)*.

D. Ogilvy, *Ogilvy on Advertising* (Prion Books, 2011).

A. Petajisto, "Active share and mutual fund performance", *Financial Analysts Journal*, v.69 (4), p.73–93 (2013).

A. Von Reibnitz, "When opportunity knocks: Cross-sectional return dispersion and active fund performance", *Critical Finance Review*, v.6 (2), p.303–356 (2017).

# CHAPTER 7

# NAVIGATING A COMPLEX WORLD

This chapter should come with a warning label for readers. I am now going to discuss areas of finance that are currently being developed, and that are often euphemistically called 'heterodox'. These are theories that contradict the perceived wisdom of how financial markets work. These ideas are not mainstream – or, dare I say, not yet mainstream?

In my view, this research provides fascinating and useful insight that investors should consider, even if it sometimes seems to directly contradict conventional wisdom about markets and investing. And if you think this means that you should not pay attention to the ideas, then I suggest you go back to Chapter 5, where I discuss investors who ignore the other side of a story.

In the spirit of respecting information that contradicts your existing beliefs, I invite you to join me on a journey to investigate structural breaks in markets, market bubbles and crashes. At the journey's conclusion, I hope to have convinced you to change the way you make forecasts and manage your investments.

# Why doesn't Delphi own the world?

In the second century BC, the Attalid kings of Pergamon donated vast sums of money to the Temple of Delphi. They erected several statues on the temple grounds, both to further their prominence amongst the Hellenic and Mediterranean people and to demonstrate their virtues as donors for the common good.

The Temple of Delphi was considered the most important temple in the ancient Greek world. Dedicated to Apollo – the Greek god of knowledge, harmony and light – it attracted people from all over the Hellenic world who, for an appropriate donation, could ask the oracle of Delphi for advice. The famously indecipherable predictions, which could apply to all kinds of scenarios, turned the oracle into the stuff of legend.

In today's language, we would say that the donations to the Temple of Delphi formed an endowment that was managed with the aim of paying for the expenses of the temple. The donations were mostly hoarded in the form of silver and the main source of income for the endowment were loans that, according to economic historians Homer and Sylla, were lent to 'safe borrowers' at an annual interest rate of 6.67%.

Given the initial endowment of silver 2000 years ago, the endowment of the Temple of Delphi would have grown to a vast sum if it had managed to lend the money at a consistent interest rate of 6.67% per year. In fact, at the current price of silver, it would be $2.14 times $10^{62}$ today. That is, $214,000,000,000,000,000,000,000,000,000,000,000,000,000,000,000,000,000,000,000,000,000,000.00.

In comparison, the number of atoms in the sun is 10,000 times smaller than that. Obviously the Temple of Delphi is not the biggest institutional investor in the world, as is it long defunct and forgotten. The moral of the story should be obvious: what works at one time might stop working, either suddenly or slowly, in the future. Investors who do not adapt to change will see their fortunes dwindle and likely end up bankrupt.

# A recent regime change in currency markets

Looking at history, we can easily identify changes in investment regimes. They are, typically, triggered by war and destruction.

In the case of the Temple of Delphi, the decline and destruction of the Greek states is what cost them their fortune. The Greek states were first defeated by the Roman Empire, which later embraced Christianity, and then the Ottoman Empire, before reverting back to Christian rule.

The loss of fortune is understandable though, it is really tricky to rebrand the Temple of Apollo to the Church of Christ, to the Mosque of Delphi and then back to the Church of Christ again. After a while, people tend to consider you an opportunist and stop visiting you.

But more subtle regime changes happen all the time. One such example is given in Figure 7.1, which shows the performance of a simple carry trade strategy in currency markets. In a carry trade, the investor borrows money in low-yielding currencies, like Japanese yen or Swiss francs, and invests the borrowed money in high-yielding currencies, like the Australian dollar or, in recent years, the US dollar.

**Figure 7.1: Performance of currency carry strategies**

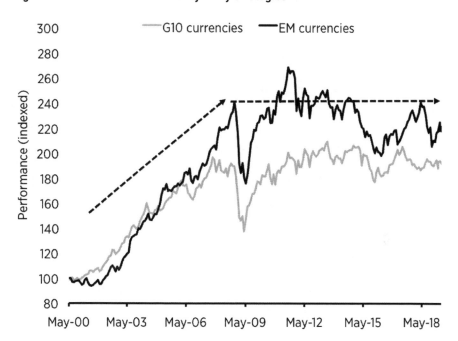

Source: Bloomberg.

The immediate benefit is that the investor pays a low rate of interest on the borrowed money (the three-month deposit rate on the Japanese yen is roughly zero at the time of writing) and receives a high rate of interest on the invested funds (the three-month deposit rate on the US dollar is roughly 2%). Of course, the risk is that the US dollar will depreciate against the Japanese yen, which may lead to a loss.

Historically, a diversified carry trade strategy, where the investor bought a basket of high-yielding currencies while borrowing a basket of low-yielding currencies, could perform extremely well in times of strong economic growth, as the high-yielding currencies appreciated.

It was only in times of crisis that those carry trades rapidly collapsed, triggering substantial losses for investors. Nevertheless, because interest rate differentials between countries tended to be large, and recessions rare, carry trade strategies worked quite well in the long run, both in the ten largest currency blocs (the so-called G10), and in emerging markets (EM), as Figure 7.1 shows.

But, in reaction to the global financial crisis of 2008, central banks in North America and Western Europe followed the Bank of Japan in cutting interest rates to zero and, in some cases, even to negative rates. As a result, the interest rate differentials that drove carry trade returns became very small, or disappeared altogether. After 2009, carry trade strategies stopped working as central banks followed a zero interest rate policy for more than a decade.

## Currency hedge funds stop performing

The impact of this regime change in carry trades reverberated throughout the world of currency hedge funds. Of course, currency hedge funds run many different strategies that are typically much more sophisticated than the simple carry trade I explained above. Yet, as Figure 7.2 shows, their performance until 2009 was often very similar to the performance of the carry trade. And just as the carry trade stopped working after the global financial crisis, so too did currency hedge funds.

**Figure 7.2: Performance of currency hedge funds**

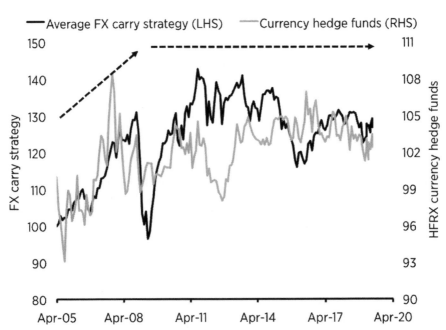

Source: Bloomberg.

The average return of currency hedge funds over the last decade has been indistinguishable from zero. Despite their sophistication and immense manpower, they have been unable to make money when interest rates on all major currencies have been the same, namely zero. In such an environment, it becomes essentially a matter of luck if a currency appreciates or depreciates relative to another currency, and so the currency hedge funds no longer had a way to make money.

Just like the Temple of Delphi declined once it became unable to make money, so have currency hedge funds today. According to BarclayHedge, the assets under management of dedicated currency trading hedge funds have declined from a peak of $37.4bn in autumn 2008 to just $13.3bn at the beginning of 2019.

# The flawed foundations of modern finance

In hindsight, it is always easy to identify the point in time when a given investment strategy stopped working. More than a decade after the global financial crisis, it has become clear that the fundamental change in monetary policy led to a fundamental change in currency markets, which would impair the ability of currency hedge funds to make money.

Other investment strategies have stopped working after the crisis as well. As I have demonstrated in Chapter 3, value stocks have underperformed growth stocks for more than a decade. The open question for many value-oriented, long-term investors, is whether value will ever start working again?

The really difficult part of investing is to identify regime changes as they happen, rather than several years, or a decade, later. If we can only detect structural shifts in how markets work with several years' delay, then the damage to the performance of the portfolio is already done and it will likely take a long time to recover from the losses. This is one reason why I was so adamant in Chapter 3 about the need to limit downside risks with the help of stop-losses and other tools discussed there.

Unfortunately, while identifying regime shifts in financial markets is of vital importance to investors, finance theory and, in particular, modern portfolio theory, do not provide any answers. I am not going to digress into a lengthy explanation of modern portfolio theory, or other mainstream theories of how financial markets work – there are plenty of good books on these topics – but I would like to mention three core assumptions that these theories make:

1. Equilibrium thinking

2. Linearity

3. Homogeneity

Let's look at these in turn.

## 1. Equilibrium thinking

The first assumption is that there is some form of equilibrium that financial markets try to achieve over time. Prices are determined by the equilibrium of demand and supply at which the highest volume of transaction is possible. If prices deviate from this equilibrium, they will, over time, feel an invisible force that pulls them back.

The only way prices can change is if the equilibrium point changes, that is, if either demand or supply, or both, changes. The price of a stock, for example, is determined by demand for and supply of the stock. As long as there is no news about the company, or the economy, neither supply nor demand is expected to change, and the price should hover within a small range.

There are some technical factors that can influence the price, such as a large investor rebalancing their portfolio and, in the process, selling some of the holdings in that company, but, in the big picture, the price of the share should remain rather stable.

Suddenly, there is news that company management is cutting costs and reducing the workforce by 10,000 people. Some investors will consider this positive news, since lower costs should lead to higher profits for shareholders. Demand for the stock will increase.

But the investors who already own the stock will likely no longer be willing to sell the stock at the old price because they, too, think that corporate profits will rise. Thus, they are only willing to sell their shares at a price that reflects the new higher valuation they put on the company.

The end result is that the share price will increase, in reaction to the news, until enough investors are willing to sell their shares to new investors. This news about the company therefore forced existing and new investors to reassess the future profits of the company and, thus, both demand and supply changed, leading to a shift in price towards a new equilibrium.

## 2. Linearity

The second fundamental assumption of modern finance theory is linearity. Put simply: more is always more, and less is always less. Let's go back to the example of the company announcing cost cuts above. Let's say that the announced cut of 10,000 staff leads to an increase in the operating margin of the company from 10% to 11%, and that this increase in operating margin triggers a jump in share price by 4%.

Imagine the company had announced a cut of 5,000 people instead of 10,000. You might guess that this leads to an increase of the operating margin from 10% to 10.5%, and to an increase in the share price of 2%. Half as many jobs cut should roughly lead to half the increase in profitability, and half the increase in the share price.

I am well aware that I am making some assumptions here that are not entirely correct, since there are fixed costs to cutting jobs and, as a result, cutting half as many people will not lead to half the gain in operating margin etc. But, as a first approximation, this linear relationship between cost cutting and share price reaction seems about right.

Now, imagine the company had announced the cut of 20,000 jobs. By the same line of argument, you would expect the share price to jump by 8%, or 16% if it cuts 40,000 jobs. But what if the company only has 40,000 employees in total? This kind of linear thinking tells us that cutting all the jobs and, thus, shutting down the company altogether would increase the share price.

Clearly, the linear relationship between cost cutting and share price breaks down at the point when the cost cutting impairs the ability of the business to operate.

You would think that this is common sense, but neither investors nor corporate executives seem to understand this all the time. Of course, everyone understands that if you cut costs so much that the business effectively has to shut down, your share price will go to zero, but, in a less extreme form, this mistake is made time and again.

One of my pet peeves in life is having to fly airlines that are American. No matter whether you fly economy, business or first class, the experience on a US-based airline is consistently worse than on a European or Asian airline. The seats are tighter, the food is worse, the entertainment programme is less varied and, though I can never put my finger on it, everything feels 'cheap', when compared to the service I get on a premium airline in Europe, the Middle East or Asia.

In my view, the reason for this lower quality is that executives in the US are beholden to the idol of cost cutting. Whenever profits decline, their first instinct is to cut costs to make the company profitable again. They cut the food menu and the entertainment system, and they cram more people into a cabin to increase revenues per flight. Everything is fair game, as long as costs are kept low. The end result is a steady decline in the quality of service.

In comparison, premium airlines, like the ones in the Middle East or East Asia, don't necessarily cut costs when they face declining profits. They argue that they can charge a premium price if they offer superior service. They focus more on the quality of service, and less on cutting costs.

The result is that, over time, travellers like me start to avoid the US-based airlines altogether and switch to the premium airlines, simply because we make our flying decisions not just based on price, but on other factors as well. Personally, I don't enjoy flying that much, so I am willing to pay a little extra to get a more comfortable flight, as well as better food and entertainment.

This difference in approach can be seen in other industries as well. The US car industry has experienced a steady decline since the 1970s because the reaction of corporate executives was, time and again, to cut costs whenever profits declined. In comparison, German and Japanese car manufacturers focused on producing a quality product that people wanted to buy, and were willing to pay a premium for.

Today, German and Japanese manufacturers dominate the car market globally, and everyone who can afford it will drive a German brand rather than an American brand. As German economy minister Sigmar Gabriel once replied to the complaint, made by US President Donald Trump, that Americans no longer buy American cars: "If they'd make better cars, people would buy them".

## 3. Homogeneity

The third assumption of modern finance that I would like to criticise, is the assumption that an average provides good guidance for investment decisions. The underlying assumption to this theme is that all the investors in the world can be represented by one 'average' investor and his beliefs.

If wages grow by 3% per year, it is assumed that everyone who has a job gets 3% more money. In reality, this is not the case. The increase in wages might be unequally distributed, with highly-skilled workers receiving a large pay rise while low-skilled workers get no increase. Over time, the income disparity will increase, even though, statistically, we all get better off on average. This rising inequality will eventually lead to significant economic consequences.

An increase in the working poor in a society leads to an increase in government spending on social safety nets. This, in turn, may lead to higher income and corporate taxes, and, subsequently, to lower profits for corporations. An increase in income inequality also results in envy and anger directed at the 1% of top earners.

These events can lead to street protests, like the Occupy Wall Street movement, and the emergence of populist politicians, such as Donald Trump. Once in power, the unconventional policies of such politicians – for example a trade war and Trump's border wall – may disrupt the business environment.

Figure 7.3 shows the Gini coefficient – the most common measure of income inequality – for different countries. While some countries, like the UK, have experienced a small decline in income inequality since the global financial crisis, the overall trend since the 1980s has been towards increased inequality in North America, Europe and Asia.

**Figure 7.3: Income inequality around the world**

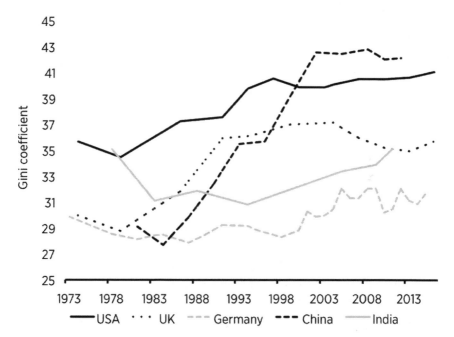

Source: Branko Milanovic database.

A similar mistake is often made by investors who try to figure out 'what the market thinks' by averaging the behaviour of many investors. The problem with this approach is that if every investor around the world thinks the same about a given stock or bond, no trade would ever be made. That's because a trade needs a buyer and a seller.

The buyer has to be convinced that the stock or bond is undervalued at that moment and will increase in price in the future. The seller, on the other hand, has to be convinced that the stock or bond is too expensive. Only the disagreement between buyer and seller creates a trade. Averaging between the seller and buyer might provide some information about the market overall, but it also ignores some important factors.

# Financial markets as complex dynamic systems

Given these shortcomings of modern finance theory, a group of renegade academics and practitioners – mostly with a background in the natural sciences and engineering – have been working on a different theory of financial markets that is more complex and dynamic. This approach looks at financial markets as an example of complex dynamic systems (duh!).

If this sounds scary and complicated, let me assure you that everyone is already familiar with a whole range of complex dynamic systems. The most prominent such system is the weather. We all know that the interaction between sunlight, water, humidity, and the shape of the land and water on the surface of the Earth, creates all kinds of interesting phenomena.

Changes in the humidity of the air can lead to the formation of clouds which, when they hit a mountain range, will create rain showers. Air that is heated up over a desert may drift out into the ocean where it collides with cold air that has been cooled by the ocean currents. Where the hot and cold air meet, it is typically going to be windy, and thunderstorms and windstorms can form. These storms, in turn, can drift back on land and devastate large areas.

Meteorologists understand that the weather is never in equilibrium. The constant change in solar radiation between day and night, and the change in absorption of solar radiation by different surfaces of the Earth, mean that there is never an equilibrium to which the weather drifts, nor can there ever be an equilibrium. The defining feature of weather is that it is dynamic, i.e., it changes all the time and never comes to a rest.

Similarly, no meteorologist would ever think of weather phenomena as linear. If the temperature in a city is twice as high today compared to a month ago, this does not mean that if it rained 3mm a month ago that it will rain 6mm today. If it were that simple, weather forecasters would have been out of a job a long time ago.

Finally, nobody would ever dream of thinking about the weather as the same everywhere. It is clear to all of us that averaging out does not provide much insight. The average temperature of the Earth is a moderate 15°C. Tell that to an Inuit in Northern Canada, or a Bedouin in the Sahara Desert. Similarly, the average annual temperature in Tokyo is also 15°C but, in January, the average temperature is 5.2°C, and in August it is 27.1°C.

Wearing the same coat all year round would make you quite uncomfortable most of the time. It would probably remind you of the old economist joke about the guy who had his head in the oven and his feet in the fridge and said: "On average, this is quite comfortable". So why do we think financial markets can be explained by an 'average' investor?

# Insights from complex dynamic systems

The study of financial markets as complex dynamic systems focuses on four key attributes which can help investors gain a deeper understanding of financial markets and their behaviour.

1. Heterogeneity

2. Nonlinearity

3. Adaptation and feedback

4. Emergence

## 1. Heterogeneity

Figure 7.4, which we first saw in Chapter 3, shows the phases of the business cycle during which value investors and momentum investors make profits. The traditional way to explain these swings of the business cycle around a long-term trend, is to assume that the long-term trend is an equilibrium, towards which the price of an asset drifts. If the price is very far away from the equilibrium, valuation forces will increasingly pull the price back towards the fundamental value. Once the price drifts towards equilibrium, the valuation force will decline and momentum will take over.

**Figure 7.4: Value and momentum investors in the cycle**

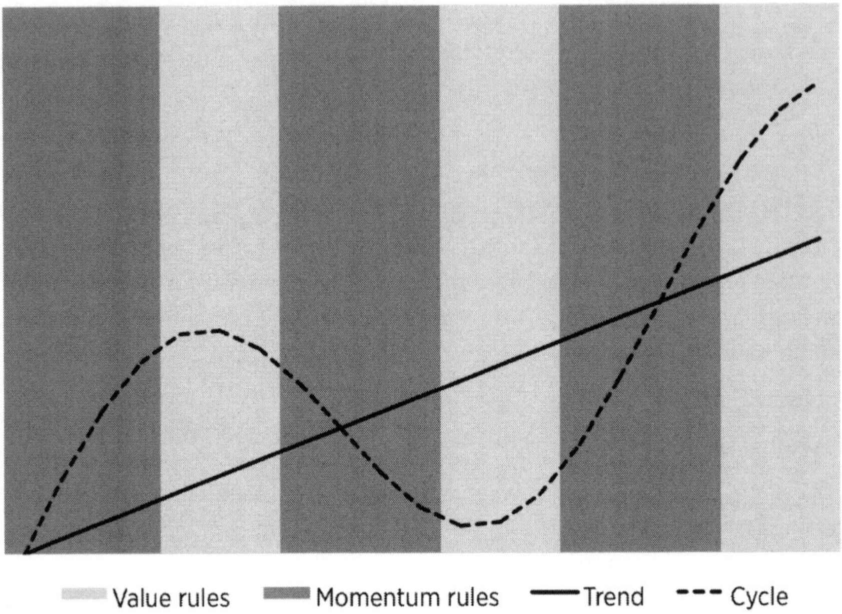

Value rules      Momentum rules      ——Trend      - - - Cycle

Source: Author.

But the question traditional finance theory cannot answer, at least not to my satisfaction, is why the price of the asset overshoots the fundamental value. If the long-term trend acts as an equilibrium, then we would expect the price to swing a few times around this fundamental value, with these swings having a declining amplitude until, eventually, the price stabilises at the fundamental value.

Instead, we observe wild swings in the markets around a fundamental value, and these swings never disappear.

Complex dynamic systems theory has a different approach to explaining these cycles. Instead of assuming an equilibrium that attracts the price like a magnet, it takes the heterogeneity of investors seriously.

Assume there are two groups of investors. The first group are value investors. They will only invest in assets that they perceive as significantly undervalued relative to their fundamental value. If the current price of the asset is somewhere near the fundamental value, they will do nothing. If the current price is significantly above the fundamental value, they will sell existing holdings or short the asset.

The second group of investors are momentum investors. They just look at the price action of an asset. If the price is moving sideways, they ignore the asset and do nothing. If the price has increased for a while, they will buy the asset and ride the existing trend. If the trend changes, and the price starts to decline, they will sell their holdings or short the asset.

Assume that the price of an asset is a little bit above the fundamental value. Value investors will ignore this small deviation, because there isn't enough margin of safety for them in the price to sell their investment. Momentum investors, however, can smell a trend forming so start buying the stock (let's assume that there is a third group of investors called market-makers, who stand ready to sell their shares to whoever wants them, in this case momentum investors).

Because the momentum investors create more demand for the shares, the price increases some more, attracting more momentum investors who, in turn, create even more demand for the asset. This feedback loop creates a rising tide for momentum investors who start to make a profit for their investors. People who delegate their investment decisions to professionals take notice, and the positive returns of the momentum investors attract additional funds. With these additional funds, the momentum investors can buy even more of the asset, driving the price even higher.

At some point, however, the price of the asset will be far enough above the fundamental value, that value investors start selling their holdings and short the asset. The higher the price, the more value investors will start to sell their holdings. This creates an increase in supply that will eventually become sufficient to overcome demand and lead to a price decline.

As prices start to decline, some momentum investors take profits by selling their holdings. This creates additional supply which pushes prices even lower. In reaction to this price decline, more momentum investors start to sell their assets, and investors who delegate their investment decisions move money from the momentum investors to the value investors.

After all, these were the managers who made the most profit, by being the first to bet against the overvalued asset. Now, we witness the feedback loop in reverse. Momentum investors sell more and more of the asset that value investors have already sold or shorted. The price drops until, eventually, it falls below the fundamental value – simply because, at the fundamental value, neither momentum investors nor value investors are willing to buy the asset.

Only once the price has dropped significantly below the fundamental value, will value investors start to buy the asset and increase demand for it. And thus, the cycle begins anew.

This discussion shows that a complex dynamic system view of the market does *not* assume that the fundamental value of an asset is an equilibrium price. Instead, it postulates that the different views of investors push prices away from the fundamental value, and then back towards it again.

It is the interplay between different investor types, the changing profitability of their strategies, and their ability to attract money from outside investors, that determines how influential the different investor types will become in the market. As the influence of one investment strategy increases, prices will behave as if they were following this strategy. But, eventually, any strategy will become so dominant that there is little to be gained by attracting additional money.

At this point, the tide turns and the investment strategy that did not work in the past will become profitable again, attracting more money – and prices will suddenly behave as if they follow that strategy.

This view of financial markets as complex dynamic systems with heterogenous investors informed the tools I proposed for managing risk as a long-term investor in Chapter 3. Remember the billiard table with the ball and the rubber bands of different length and strength? This is effectively what is happening in complex dynamic systems. Different groups of investors with different investment strategies look at the same situation from different angles.

Most of the time, they have little incentive to buy or sell an asset. But, there comes a point when the incentive to buy or sell an asset becomes overwhelming for one group of investors. That is the point when one of the rubber bands is stretched and starts to pull the ball in a different direction. And that is when the price of the asset starts to behave differently.

## 2. Nonlinearity

The previous paragraph also shows why financial markets are not linear. If we assume that momentum investors and value investors both follow simple linear rules to buy and sell an asset, nothing would change.

If, for example, momentum investors invest 1% of their portfolio in an asset that has rallied 5%, and 2% of their portfolio in an asset that has rallied 10%, etc., and value investors invest 1% of their portfolio into assets that are 10% undervalued, and 2% of their portfolio into assets that are 20% undervalued, etc., nothing in the dynamics of the markets would change. We would still get the swings and cycles in financial markets.

But the price dynamics of the asset become increasingly nonlinear in this kind of market, because once an investment strategy has been successful for a while, it attracts additional investments. And these additional investments are then invested into the same asset, pushing prices even higher.

The end result is a snowball effect that leads to faster and faster price acceleration, both to the upside and the downside. In well-behaved cases, the price of the asset will rise exponentially, but, in some cases, a bubble can form when prices grow faster than exponential growth and go through the roof (or floor). In the section below, on emergence, I will show how asset bubbles can be identified by looking for this kind of nonlinear behaviour in prices.

There are also situations when nonlinear behaviour suddenly appears out of nowhere in financial markets. Let us go back to the global financial crisis of 2008; one of the many things that went horribly wrong was the reliance of investors on their ability to sell assets whenever they wanted.

However, as one bank after another got into trouble, banks were increasingly unwilling to lend to other banks, because nobody knew if the other bank would be able to survive the next day. Suddenly, what started as a credit crunch for banks, turned into a global liquidity crunch.

Several assets that were constantly traded over the counter between different banks and investors suddenly could not be sold anymore. Banks who routinely kept the riskiest tranches of mortgage CDOs on their balance sheets, to sell them on to institutional investors at a later stage, could no longer sell these assets. And without any buyers, these assets effectively became worthless for the banks, creating massive losses that led to the bankruptcy, or near-bankruptcy, of some of the biggest lenders in the world.

What we witnessed in 2008 was what physicists and meteorologists call a phase transition. If you cool water, there comes a point, at 0°C, when it turns to ice. What used to be a liquid is now a solid, and this solid form of water has vastly different properties than its liquid state. A similar transition occurs when a company cuts costs too much. There comes a point when additional cost cutting prevents the company from functioning effectively, and management has put the company on the path to bankruptcy.

Monetary policy over the last decade or so has also experienced such a phase transition. By cutting interest rates to zero, engaging in quantitative easing, and other unconventional measures, the central banks have essentially abandoned traditional monetary policy and transformed it into something that behaves quite differently from monetary policy in the past.

For example, over the last decade, lower interest rates have not boosted inflation in Europe and North America in the same way it has done in the past. Similarly, economic recovery was quite weak compared to previous cycles, while asset prices have been boosted to extreme valuation levels – all in reaction to these unconventional monetary policy measures.

Many economists and market pundits fear that these unconventional monetary policy measures will lead to excessive inflation or market crashes in the future. In my view, they are making a crucial mistake. They assume that current monetary policy can be compared in its effects to the past.

They implicitly assume that quantitative easing, and other measures, are linear phenomena that are essentially more of the same of what we did in the past. However, monetary policy after the global financial crisis is qualitatively different from monetary policy before it. Thus, we cannot say with any degree of confidence that these unconventional policy measures will have the same consequences, namely, market crashes or excessive inflation.

The true answer is that we simply don't know how these experiments will end. And that is, possibly, an even scarier assessment of the current situation than the doomsday scenarios of these pundits, because it also means that we will have no idea how to save the global economy from potentially catastrophic unintended consequences.

So far, things have turned out well, but absolutely nobody can say what the future holds in this area. And this is an important thing for investors to remember.

## 3. Adaptation and feedback

As humans, we tend to believe in the simple relationship between cause and effect. If I go to the office on a Monday morning and punch my boss in the face, I will lose my job by Monday evening. If I start my new job by going to my new boss and punching him in the face, I will lose my job there too. Cause and effect. You punch your boss, you lose your job. It is simple and, in most circumstances, it helps us navigate our environment quite well.

But there are situations when things aren't that simple. We humans are not robots. We constantly learn to adapt to our environment based on the feedback we get. Change the environment and we change our behaviour. The behaviour of Inuit in Northern Canada is vastly different from the behaviour of an office worker in Hong Kong, or a bushman in the Kalahari. Their behaviour differs because their environment differs; they have developed a lifestyle that is most effective and convenient in their specific environment.

As part of the global tribe of office workers, I will never forget my first visit to my sister-in-law, who lives at the edge of civilisation in Alaska. When I arrived at her village, she asked me to chop some firewood for the night with a blunt hatchet. It took me less than two minutes to slip and almost cut off my left thumb.

The reason why I will never forget this incident is because I am looking at the scar on my thumb as I type these words. The feedback I got from the hatchet was strong enough for me to change my behaviour and never use one again.

I am maladapted to life in the wilderness of Alaska but, if I was forced to stay there long enough, I would learn the necessary skills and stop some of my habits I have as a city slicker. Either that, or I'd be mauled to death by a bear.

In financial markets, the same processes of adaptation and feedback can be observed. If investors made money with one kind of investment, they tend to make similar investments again. This is called reinforcement learning. If we get a good outcome, we do more of it. If we get a poor outcome, we stop doing it.

Recall Chapter 4, where I talked about how our experiences influence our investment decisions. I showed that investors tend to stick to the kind of investments that have worked for them in the past. But, as the world around them changes, the old ways of investing may stop working. Most of the time, they only work a little less than before, so investors ignore the feedback that markets give them, and continue to do the same things that they have always done.

These are the situations where investment diaries, and the other tools I describe in that chapter, can help investors learn faster and adapt to a changing market.

In some instances, however, the feedback is very strong and behaviour changes immediately; so much so, that it may cause a traumatic memory that lasts a lifetime. As I said above, I used the hatchet in Alaska only once, and haven't touched one since. That is an adaptation of my behaviour to the extreme feedback I got from the hatchet (obviously, it was all the hatchet's fault).

Imagine an investor who starts investing a few years before the global financial crisis. This person may have invested in the stock market but, as the crisis hit, lost half or more of their investments. This loss can be so intense that the investor changes their behaviour and shuns stocks altogether afterwards. Instead, this investor will focus their portfolio on safe investments, like government bonds or gold.

I started my career as an investor in the heyday of the tech bubble in the late 1990s. The subsequent losses in technology stocks, from 2000 to 2003, made me a lifetime sceptic of technology stocks, and the promises of technology companies to revolutionise the world. For many years, I have shunned technology stocks in my personal portfolio. Only through the analysis of my investment diary did I learn that I overcompensated for my early experiences as an investor.

Since then, I have learned to work around this 'maladaptation' by creating feedback loops in my investment process (through the use of checklists) that have helped me embrace these assets. Today, I own technology stocks in my portfolio, but in a very selective way that is informed by what I learned from the tech bubble, my investment diary, and analysis of the new crop of technology companies in recent years.

That extreme events can have a lasting impression on many investors, and financial markets overall, can be seen from the research of Michael Ehrmann and Panagiota Tzamourani from the European Central Bank and the Bank of Greece, respectively. They looked at surveys of 52,000 people in 23 countries from 1981 to 2000. A part of these surveys asked how important the respondents considered the fight against high inflation to be. Figure 7.5 shows the percentage of respondents who put the fight against inflation as first or second priority for policy makers.

**Figure 7.5: Memories of high inflation**

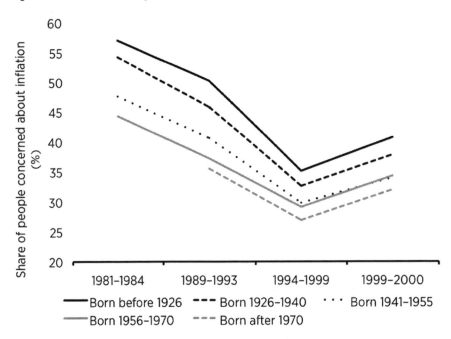

Source: Ehrmann and Tzamourani (2012).

The first thing to notice is that, in the early 1980s, memories of the high inflation of the late 1970s, and all the economic problems that came with it, were still fresh. As a result, the majority of respondents considered the fight against inflation as a top priority. But even ten years after inflation was tamed, in the late 1980s and early 1990s, about half the respondents still put the fight against inflation as a top priority. It took until the late 1990s to 'forget' the experience of the 1970s and stop worrying about inflation.

The second effect to notice in Figure 7.5 is that older respondents were systematically more afraid of inflation than younger respondents. This can be explained by looking at their lifetime experiences of inflation. The oldest generation in the sample consisted of people born before 1926. These respondents had a vivid memory not only of the high inflation of the 1970s, but of the inflationary and, in some cases, hyperinflationary periods after the Second World War (e.g. Hungary), or before and during the Great Depression (e.g. Weimar Germany).

They had learned the devastating effects high inflation can have on an economy several times in their lives and, thus, were rightfully scared of it. The youngest generation in the sample consisted of people born after 1970. During their lifetime, their only experience of inflation was during the 1970s and, in most cases, were too young to understand the effects.

Today, most of the respondents in the two oldest generations are dead, which explains why high inflation is a non-issue for the majority of investors. Most people simply never experienced the 1970s inflation, and the ones that did have grown old by now.

Forty years after the end of the last episode of high inflation, we have two generations of investors who never had to worry about inflation. No wonder financial markets act as if inflation is not an issue. Adaptation and feedback did their job once again and, in this case, created a lack of concern about rising inflation and its impact on financial markets.

## 4. Emergence

The last emphasis of complex dynamic systems research is that the combination of the previous three effects (heterogeneity, nonlinearity and adaptation) leads to the emergence of new market regimes seemingly out of nowhere. On any one day, financial markets can be behaving in a rational and calm manner until, literally overnight, events spiral out of control.

If you follow modern finance theory, this should not happen. This is because, supposedly, markets are always drifting towards an equilibrium, and this equilibrium can only shift by a large amount if there is a sizeable shift in demand or supply. But, in a complex dynamic system, there is no equilibrium. Complex dynamic systems are always changing, and small causes can spiral into large effects.

In meteorology, this is known as the butterfly effect. Discovered by Edward Lorenz, this theory asserts that minute variations in the original state of a system can lead to vastly different outcomes at a later stage. Metaphorically speaking, the flapping wings of a butterfly in the US can trigger a thunderstorm in China.

To see how a very different behaviour of financial markets can emerge, seemingly out of nowhere, it is worthwhile looking at the work of Didier Sornette, a professor of finance and entrepreneurial risk at the Federal Institute of Technology in Zurich, Switzerland. Sornette started his career studying earthquakes, another complex dynamic system, but switched to financial markets.

His work has focused, among other things, on detecting market bubbles in real time and trying to forecast when the bubble will lead to a crash. As you might guess, this is research in progress, and you should not expect that he and his team are able to forecast the timing of market crashes just yet. But they are making progress by monitoring certain characteristics that markets display in the run-up to a bubble.

Didier Sornette, and other researchers, have observed two phenomena. First, financial markets tend to be well behaved most of the time. This means that advances and declines happen at moderate speeds and follow an exponential growth process. This exponential growth process is essentially the compound interest process that savers experience in their savings account.

Assume your savings account pays 5% interest per year. If you put $100 in your savings account, you will have $105.00 after one year. After two years, you will have $110.25 – the original $105, plus $5 interest on $100 invested at the beginning, and $0.25 interest on the $5 interest earned in the first year. After three years, you will have $115.76, and so on.

However, in an asset bubble, prices grow faster than this exponential rate. They exhibit hyperbolic growth. Classic examples are share prices that increase by 10% after some news breaks. The next day, they go up by 20%, then by 50%, then by 100% etc. Instead of having a relatively stable rate of return, the rate of return itself grows exponentially fast and the chart of the asset's price seems to almost fall over backwards.

The second effect researchers observed is so-called log-periodicity. As I have explained in the section on heterogeneity, there is a constant struggle between buyers and sellers of an asset. This interplay between different groups of investors leads to the cycles we observe in markets. On a smaller timescale, we can observe such cycles in asset prices. Share prices don't advance uniformly, but in waves; they advance sharply, just to drop a little bit, then stabilise before another advance begins etc.

What happens is that momentum investors buy the asset and drive its price higher. After a while, some momentum investors may want to take profits and sell some, or all, of their holdings. This is when demand for the asset temporarily declines and the price drops a little. After the price drops sufficiently, some investors will see this as an opportunity to 'buy the dip'. Demand increases again, and the asset price rises once more.

Normally, this buy-the-dip mentality is not the dominating force in the market, but, in a bubble, it becomes the all-encompassing narrative. Investors see the strong return of an asset in the past and fear they might miss out on the rally. So, they use a dip to buy into the asset. If enough investors do this, the recovery after the dip will be even stronger than the previous advance. This, in turn, attracts even more investors when the next dip arrives, and so on.

The result is that momentum investors buy the dip, and sell to take profits, in faster and faster cycles. Dips become shorter and advances more vigorous as the bubble forms. Of course, eventually there comes a point when there are no more investors left in the market willing to buy the dip and make a quick profit. This is when the bubble pops and the price starts to decline. By this time, there is a large number of investors holding an asset that they bought at highly inflated prices. This leads to a mad rush for the exit and a sudden, almost immediate, collapse in price – a crash.

Figure 7.6 shows this emergence of a bubble for the Dow Jones Industrial Average Index in the year before the stock market crash of October 1987. The example is adapted from Didier Sornette's research. The figure shows that, throughout most of 1986, the Dow Jones was well behaved, with a relatively benign rally in the first half of the year, and a sideways movement in the second.

**Figure 7.6: Log-periodic behaviour of the Dow Jones Industrial Average before the 1987 crash**

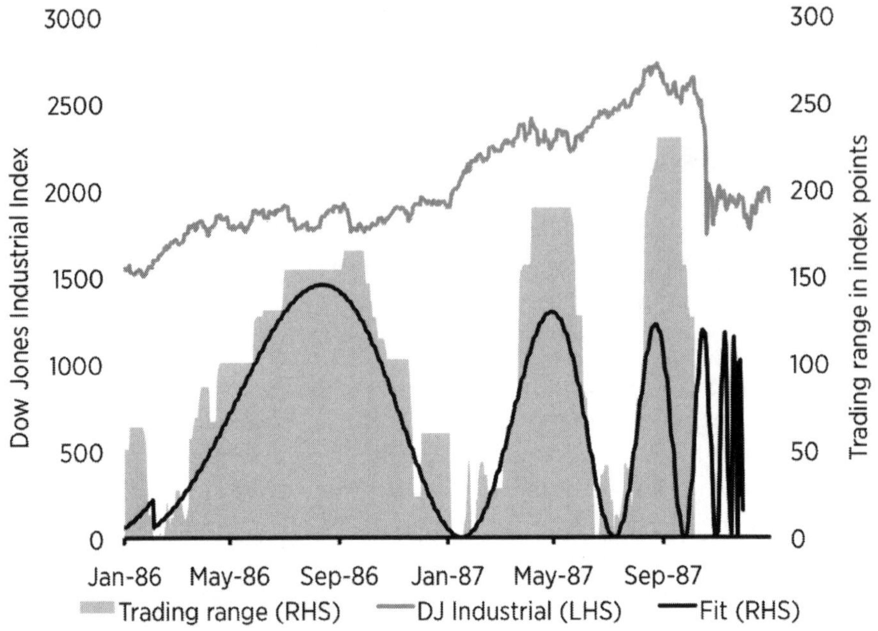

Source: Sornette (2002).

The grey area in Figure 7.6 shows the trading range of the Dow Jones over the previous 12 months. As the index moved sideways in the second half of 1986, the trading range narrowed, before expanding again in early 1987. The advance in the Dow Jones was now much stronger. More investors wanted to participate in the rally, so when the Dow Jones dipped a little in summer 1987, investors were quick to buy into it and push prices even higher.

This time, the advance was even stronger, but it lasted only until September, when it dipped again. As before, more investors tried to jump onto the bandwagon. Unfortunately, there weren't enough investors left who were willing or able to buy the dip, and the entire market started to collapse.

What started as a relatively moderate decline on Wednesday, 14 October 1987, accelerated to a 108-point decline (4.6%) on Friday, 16 October 1987. The decline happened on record volume, indicating that a lot of investors wanted to sell as quickly as possible, leading US Treasury Secretary James Baker to show concern about the market decline.

By the following Monday, there was no stopping anymore. Starting in Asian markets, and accelerating throughout European trading hours, the Dow Jones

Industrial Average dropped hundreds of points within minutes, as investors rushed for the exits. At the end of the day, the index had fallen a further 508 points, or 22.6% – still the largest one-day decline ever recorded.

More than 30 years after the Black Monday of 1987, modern finance theory still cannot explain what caused the market to crash by that much. In fact, the basic tenets of modern finance theory state that such a drop should happen maybe once in billions of years. Yet, financial markets crash time and again, and far more often than modern finance theory predicts.

With the help of complex dynamic systems research, we will hopefully come one step closer to explaining when such crashes happen and how to prepare for them. If we are extremely lucky, we might even one day be able to predict market crashes before they happen. But I am not hopeful.

After all, if we could reliably predict market crashes before they happen, investors would adapt to this knowledge, change their behaviour, and potentially never create a bubble to begin with. And while this may sound like a good thing, in practice, such investor adaptation would lead to a change in market behaviour, which would subsequently turn the prediction false. Therefore, as a result of the prediction, it would again become impossible to predict the market.

Alternatively, they might adapt in such a way that they try to benefit from a crash. In this case, the crash would happen earlier than predicted, simply because more and more investors would buy derivatives to benefit from the coming crash, or sell their investments earlier than they would have done.

Financial markets display what investment legend George Soros calls "reflexivity". They constantly adapt to the views of investors, changing their behaviour as investors change theirs. This creates another round of changes in investor behaviour which, in turn, changes the behaviour of markets. It is a constant, dynamic process, never in equilibrium, and forever unpredictable.

## How to think about markets as systems

Thinking about markets as complex dynamic systems is, in my view, a promising direction for research that will enable us to better understand why markets act the way they do. It is also a challenge to us investors, because it requires us to think very differently about markets.

For one, we need to abolish the linear 'if… then…' style of thinking, which dominates investment strategies today. As we have seen above, markets are well-behaved most of the time, but they can suddenly, and seemingly without cause, shift into extreme behaviour. Thus, as investors, we need to practise thinking in terms of feedback loops and adaptation.

Figure 7.7 illustrates how complex this can get. In a linear world, as it is described by modern finance theory, we can simply say that if A happens, then so will B. For example, if a stock is undervalued versus the market by 20%, it should outperform the market in the next few years. Or, if the central bank cuts interest rates, then the economy gets a boost.

**Figure 7.7: Thinking in feedback loops**

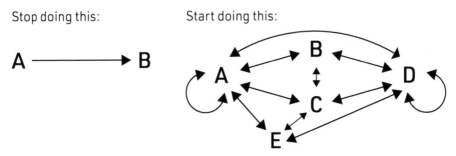

Source: Author.

Instead, what might happen is that B feeds back to A and influences C and D, while A influences C, D and E. Meanwhile, E influences C and D, and C and D influence B. And so on. That might make your head spin, but financial markets are way more complicated than we like to believe.

To give you an example of these feedback loops, let's think about the above statement that if the central bank cuts interest rates, the economy gets a boost. You might say this is common sense and at the heart of monetary policy. If interest rates get cut by the central bank, then commercial banks will be able to provide cheaper loans to businesses, and cheaper mortgages to private households.

This, in turn, means that businesses will take out loans to invest in future growth and households will buy bigger homes, or re-mortgage their existing home and spend the additional money on renovating their property. All of these actions lead to stronger economic growth, and the anticipation of stronger economic growth means that stocks rally, as do some cyclical commodities like oil and industrial metals.

If A, then B. If the central bank cuts rates, the economy will strengthen. If the economy strengthens, stocks rally.

But let's think about the central bank cutting interest rates in a more realistic model of the world. One where we include the amount of existing debt of households and businesses. If businesses and households already own a lot of debt, cutting interest rates might still lead to lower interest on business loans and mortgages.

But, commercial banks will only lend to homeowners and businesses if they can be reasonably sure they will get their money back. If they think that a borrower might not pay back a loan, they will either not lend the money, or they will ask for higher interest in order to earn a risk premium. If some of these risky loans default, the additional interest earned will make up for the losses. After all, commercial banks aren't the Salvation Army, they are in the business of making money.

When businesses and households are already highly indebted, additional debt might get so expensive that the increase in the cost of interest might outpace the benefits of the increased consumption. This is particularly true for households that decide to increase their mortgage and spend the additional money, not on investments like the renovation of a kitchen, but on short-term consumption, like a vacation. After the vacation is over, the debt is still there and the household can consume less than before.

Similar effects may happen in businesses, where cheap loans may incentivise them to invest in dubious projects that may never become profitable, or that have such low profitability that their return doesn't even cover the cost of interest. The result is declining business profitability.

Where these last two phenomena happen on a large scale, cutting interest rates by the central bank might suddenly become counterproductive. While there might be a short-term boost to the economy from additional loans and mortgages, the medium-term effects are even lower growth for the economy. Of course, modern economic theory then dictates that the central bank should cut interest rates even more to stimulate growth. But if the central bank has already cut interest rates to zero, what can it do?

We know the answer to this: engage in quantitative easing through the large-scale buying of government bonds. This pushes the interest rates for loans even lower in the market.

So, traditional monetary policy, which worked so well since the 1980s, not only has stopped working, but becomes counterproductive. The more central banks cut interest rates, the worse economic growth will get because, in the presence of crushing debt mountains, additional loans will lead, in the medium turn, to significantly increased costs that reduce consumption and corporate profitability.

The unfortunate corollary to this is that there is no way out of this negative feedback loop. Imagine for a moment that central banks stopped cutting interest rates and stopped buying government bonds. They might even think about hiking interest rates in an effort to make loans more expensive. Because households and businesses are already saddled with so much debt, they may stop asking for more loans, but the loans that mature will have to be refinanced at a significantly higher interest rate.

This will cut the profitability of businesses even more and cut the disposable income of households. The result is lower investments, lower consumption and, thus, lower economic growth. You see that all of a sudden, we are in a situation where monetary policy is doomed. Cutting interest rates doesn't help, and hiking interest rates makes things worse. Central banks have effectively rendered themselves unable to manage the economy or inflation.

Students of economic history may know that the argument I make here is similar to the Real Bills Doctrine, which was the dominating guideline for monetary policy in the early decades of the 20th century. Simply put, the Real Bills Doctrine stated that central banks should only expand the monetary base as long as it is covered by an appropriate amount of safe assets (e.g. gold).

The idea was that, if the central bank increased the money supply too much, it would increase speculation and incentivise an unproductive use of resources. This would then undermine long-term economic growth and the overall stability of the economy. In order to prevent the central bank from expanding the money supply too much, and triggering such a wave of speculative and unproductive investment, economists thought they needed to link the money supply to a resource that the central bank could not expand at will, e.g. the amount of gold in their vaults. Because you can't create gold out of nothing, and the global supply of gold only grows slowly, this gold standard prevented the central bank from printing too much money.

The Real Bills Doctrine is today discredited because it likely contributed to the severity of the Great Depression in the 1930s. This is because when the economy shrank, investors went to the central bank and demanded their money be converted into gold. Thus, when the economy faltered at the beginning of the Great Depression, the central bank had to reduce money supply and thus cut businesses and households off from vital credit. In response, businesses and households had to cut back on consumption and investments, which made the economic decline even worse.

Today, no serious economist is advocating for this style of monetary policy. But, in my view, while the Real Bills Doctrine was too strict, we should not throw the baby out with the bath water. In fact, I believe there might be an element of truth in the Real Bills Doctrine which is worth salvaging from the ruins of the theory. And today, we might be closer to a tipping point in monetary policy than we think.

Thinking in these feedback loops is hard work, but whoever said investing is easy had no clue. The best way to incorporate dynamic systems thinking into your own way of thinking about markets, is to think about the ball on the billiards table, shown again in Figure 7.8.

**Figure 7.8: Dealing with complex dynamic systems**

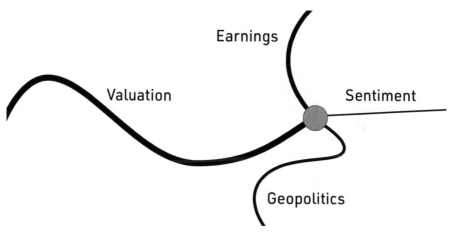

Source: Author.

We used this to think about stock markets, but you can label the rubber bands differently to deal with interest rates. For example, you could replace valuation with monetary policy rate; earnings with inflation; geopolitics with exchange rate; and sentiment with debt level. You could add other rubber bands labelled unemployment, trust in the central bank, political influence, etc.

The point is that this mental model is very flexible. All you have to do is think about what could influence an investment and how strong you think this influence is, relative to the other factors. Then you have to start looking at the data and begin to identify the ranges where the respective rubber bands have historically become stretched. Finally, you can compare the current situation with these historic extremes to try and determine if the rubber band is stretched enough to pull the ball in a different direction.

If it isn't, then forget about that rubber band for now and move to the next, until you find one that is stretched enough to move the market. If none of the rubber bands are stretched enough at the moment, chances are the ball will continue to do whatever it has done in the recent past.

Of course, complex dynamic systems may suddenly shift into a different mode and a new market regime may emerge seemingly out of nothing. This is when comparison of the historic ranges when rubber bands become stretched break down. And this is why I like stop-losses and other risk management tools. In the end, you have to respect the market. Trying to bet against the market is a dangerous game because, as we all know, markets can stay (seemingly) irrational longer than any investor can stay solvent.

In a complex dynamic system, what seems irrational can in fact be very rational, as it may be the reflection of nonlinear relationships in markets and the adaptation of investors to these relationships. Thus, risk management becomes even more important in such dynamically changing markets.

Since markets never move towards equilibrium, there is little hope of being able to predict the long-term outcome of a market development. Instead, investors have to become more humble in their ability to forecast markets. While markets should behave in one way or another, based on modern finance theory, they may deviate from this ideal behaviour for a long time.

In those cases, investors need to be able to cut losing positions in order to survive long enough to reach their long-term financial goals. Essentially, risk management becomes a strategy to survive and be able to invest again, when markets may be more conducive to your personal style of investing.

## Main points

- Markets change all the time. Sometimes these changes are small, but, at other times, they may be dramatic and last for so long that they can drive investors to ruin.

- Modern finance theory is typically unable to explain, let alone predict, these changes in market behaviour, because it is built on three core assumptions: that markets tend towards an equilibrium state; that cause and effect are linear; and that investors can be represented by taking an average of investor behaviour. All three of these assumptions have severe limitations in real markets.

- Complex dynamic systems theory looks at markets in a different way. It assumes that there are different investors with different beliefs. The interaction between these different investors is what drives markets. There are nonlinear effects in markets where a small change in one variable can lead to an exponential shift in another variable. Furthermore, investors adapt to the changing market environment, and these adaptations, in turn, influence how markets behave. All these features together can lead to the emergence of new market regimes, seemingly without cause.

- Investors need to learn to think about financial markets as complex dynamic systems. This requires practice, since thinking in feedback loops and adaptation is far more complex than the traditional ways of thinking investors are used to.

- It also means that risk management becomes far more important than it was in the view of modern finance theory. If markets are less predictable than modern finance theory assumes, and can spin out of control almost without warning, the only thing that can help investors survive in the long run is effective risk management, which will help investors to avoid losses that are so big they cannot be recovered.

# References

M. Ehrmann and P. Tzamourani, "Memories of High Inflation", *European Journal of Political Economics*, v.28 (2), p.174–191 (2012).

S. Homer and R. Sylla, *A History of Interest Rates,* 4th edition (Wiley & Sons, 2005).

D. Sornette, *Why Stock Markets Crash: Critical Events in Complex Financial Systems*, (Princeton University Press, 2002).

# CHAPTER 8

## OVER
## TO YOU

By now, I think some of you may have a very long list of complaints about this book. Everyone knows that past performance is no guarantee of future outcome but, then again, we cannot rely on forecasts either. We should not be too short-term oriented and trade too much, but neither should we be too stubborn and stick to a losing investment for too long. The markets are constantly changing and what has worked in the past may suddenly stop working. Yet, you tell us that we should learn from past experiences to increase investment success. And so on.

There are a lot of seemingly contradictory observations and recommendations in this book. However, as I pointed out at the beginning, the selection of mistakes is rather eclectic because they are based on my personal experience as both an investor and adviser. Not everybody makes all of the mistakes described in this book (well, except maybe me), nor do we make these mistakes all the time.

That's why this collection of common mistakes is only the start. Next, you'll need to adapt the recommendations for your personal needs – this will require a little introspection.

# Get to know yourself

The first, and most important, step to becoming a better investor is to take an honest look at your investments and your personality as an investor. The best way to do this is to look at past investments. Go back and look at your portfolio. Are there any systematic biases or tendencies? This can be both positive and negative.

If you do not already identify with a specific investment strategy or philosophy, you might want to check if you are more of a growth-oriented or value-oriented investor, if you are more of a trader or someone who sticks with investments for many years. Are you more driven by macroeconomic events and stock fundamentals, or price action and technical signals?

There is no right or wrong answer. As I said in Chapter 7, what makes markets tick is the divergence of opinion, and the interaction between different types of investors. Thus, all kinds of different investment approaches can lead to success. Don't let anyone tell you that chart analysis does not work, or that value is dead. If you look at financial markets as complex dynamic systems, you know that there are no such absolutes. In fact, in my career, I have met people who are consistently successful with chart analysis, macro-driven investing, value investing and a pure, quant-driven approach. If you do it right, you can be successful.

However, what I also see too often is that investors switch from one philosophy to another, or constantly chase the latest trend in investing. Often, these investors lose faith in their current investment approach after a short period of underperformance or losses.

One company I used to work for checked how often private investors changed the investment risk profile that determined their strategic asset allocation. They found that, on average, it happened every 18 months. This is a deadly mistake, as an investment strategy is something that needs to prove itself over five years or more. Changing it after one and a half years is clearly too short-term oriented. There is no investment approach that I know of that can be assessed over such a short time frame, or that can be expected to work over such a time frame all the time.

So, if you don't have an investment strategy yet, look at your portfolio and see if you can identify some tendencies in your investments. These tendencies might give you an idea of what kind of investment philosophy you are most drawn to. Most private investors, and certainly all professional investors, already have a specific investment philosophy they try to implement. Once you have a certain investment philosophy or strategy, your job is to look at your past investments and identify things you did well and things you did not do so well.

For example, if you follow a value investment style, the requirements for success are to be able to deviate from the herd and position yourself against current market trends. If you don't feel comfortable being a contrarian – an outsider in the eyes of mainstream investors – you will not be able to summon the patience and grit necessary to hold on to a value investment as markets go through boom phases.

If you are able to hold on to investments for a long time, even as market sentiment is seemingly moving against you, be aware that there are risks to holding on for too long. So, look at your past investments and see if your discipline in selling investments is as good as your discipline in holding on to them. Did you fall into value traps in the past? If so, what techniques in this book can help you avoid these traps in the future?

On the other hand, you might be a more trading-oriented investor, who relies a lot on trend-following techniques and chart analysis. If this is the case, you should be able to emotionally disconnect yourself from your investments and not get too attached to your portfolio. If you don't, you might hang on to a losing investment for too long as it accumulates losses.

If you want to marry your investments, you are likely going to be a bad trader. However, if you are able to get in and out of investments quickly, without much regret, you need to remember that there are risks to overtrading, and that transaction costs can quickly eat up your profits in the long run.

Furthermore, a common mistake of chart analysis is to use different indicators and trading patterns at different times. You might buy an asset because it breaks through resistance, with the goal of selling it once it reaches the next resistance level, but once you are there, argue that the asset isn't overbought yet because the RSI indicator is only at a reading of 50.

Consistency is the key and switching from one indicator to another is likely to cost you a lot of money at some point in the future. In fact, what you are doing is falling prey to confirmation bias, so you might want to go back to Chapter 5 and read about the techniques I described there.

# Improve yourself

Once you have identified your investment philosophy, and have a basic understanding of your strengths and weaknesses as an investor, it is time to implement a learning and self-improvement loop in your investment process. In my experience, it is advantageous to start with an investment checklist that describes the basic steps you make before any investment decision.

In the beginning, this investment checklist will likely be very short, but, over time, it will become more granular and detailed. The way to improve yourself and your investment success has been described in Chapter 4. The interplay between an investment checklist and an investment diary leads to a constant evolution of your investment approach. Every investment decision you make will help you get to know yourself a little better, as well as understand your strengths and weaknesses.

If you use investment diaries and investment checklists properly, then your investment process should gradually shift towards a process that emphasises your strengths and limits the negative impact of your weaknesses. But, don't expect that you will be able to eliminate your weaknesses or avoid mistakes altogether. That is simply not possible.

As I showed in Chapter 7, markets change all the time, which means that you will inevitably invest in assets that will lose money. If you can't live with that, then maybe investing doesn't suit you. You may be better served by handing your money to a professional, who will try to manage it for you as best they can.

# My rules for forecasting

To give you an idea of how this evolution looks, let me show you how my investment checklist for forecasts has developed over time. As I discussed in Chapter 1, forecasts over time frames of one year or so tend to be highly unreliable, and the accuracy of any forecast you can make in financial markets is much lower than you might expect it to be.

Of course, at the beginning of my career, I thought I could make forecasts for stocks – so I made the same mistake as most analysts and investors. After a while, I recognised how futile this was; that no matter how sophisticated my models would become, the uncertainty around my forecasts would still be enormous. So, I took a step back, and started with a simple checklist on how to make forecasts.

My primary rule is:

**Do not make point forecasts, only directional forecasts.**

Or, as someone once put it: "You should only forecast what is going to happen or when something is going to happen, but not both at the same time." The rule I started with was very crude and in need of improvement. So, as I made forecasting mistakes, I noted them down in my investment diary. When I came to check my diary once a year, I used this information to amend and revise my forecasting rule a little bit.

On top of that, I read great books on forecasting that provided additional insights. After years of tinkering with my forecasting rules, they currently look like this (I have added a few explanations to each rule for clarity):

1.  **Data matters**. We humans are drawn to anecdotes and illustrations – but looks can be deceiving. Always base your forecasts on data, not on qualitative arguments. Euclid's *Elements* was the first book on geometry, yet it does not have a single drawing in it.

    **Corollary A**: Torture the data until it confesses, but don't fit the data to the story.

    **Corollary B**: Start with base rates (i.e. the historical average rate at which an event happens). The assumption that nothing changes, and an event is as likely in the future as it was in the past, is a good starting point, but not the end point. Adjust this base rate with the information you have at the moment.

2.  **Don't make extreme forecasts**. Predicting the next financial crisis will make you famous if you do it at the right time, but will cost you money and your reputation in any other instance. Remember, there are only two kinds of forecasts: lucky and wrong.

3. **Reversion to the mean is a powerful force**. In economics, as well as in politics, extremes cannot survive for long. People trend towards averages, while competitive forces in business lead to mean reversion.

4. **We are creatures of habit**. If something has worked in the past, people will keep on repeating it almost forever. This introduces long-lasting trends. Don't expect these trends to change quickly, even though there is mean reversion. It is incredible how long a broken system can survive – just think of Japan.

5. **We rarely fall off a cliff**. People often change their habits at the last minute before a catastrophe happens. Yet, for behavioural change to happen, the catastrophe must be salient, the outcome must be certain and the solution must be simple.

6. **A full stomach does not riot**. Revolutions and riots rarely happen when people have enough food and feel relatively safe. A lack of personal freedom is insufficient to create revolutions, but lack of food or medicine, or injustice, all are. The Tiananmen Square revolt in China was triggered by higher food prices that students couldn't afford. The Arab Spring was also triggered by food inflation.

7. **The first goal of political and business leaders is to stay in power**. Viewed through that lens, many actions can easily be predicted.

8. **The second goal of political and business leaders is to get rich**. Combined with the previous rule, this explains about 90% of all behaviour.

9. **Remember Occam's razor**. The simplest explanation is the most likely to be correct. Ignore conspiracy theories.

10. **Don't follow rules blindly**. The world changes all the time, so be aware that any rule might suddenly stop working for a while, or even forever.

# Never stop learning

Continuous improvement will tailor your investment process to your strengths and weaknesses and, in the long run, you will end up with an investment process that fits you and only you. It will be like a bespoke suit or dress: it will look great on you and miserable on everybody else. It will make you feel truly special.

But don't expect this process of continuous self-improvement to ever stop. The moment you stop improving, you are vulnerable to changes in markets and becoming stuck in the past. You might want to review Chapters 4 and 7 to see what this can lead to in your investment portfolio.

Part of the joy of investing is that there is always something new to learn, and that, although some mistakes are common, the remedies and tools to avoid them change all the time. If I had written this book five or ten years ago, I would have given you different advice, recommending different tools and techniques. And I am sure that if I write this book in five or ten years, the recommendations would differ again. What I have done here is give you the best advice I can with my current knowledge and experience.

I make no guarantees that the tools and techniques discussed here work all the time, but I can assure you that they have helped to make me a better investor. I am pretty confident that these tools and techniques will work for you as well, because I am not special. I am not an investment genius, or supremely skilled. I am not particularly rational as an investor, nor am I particularly skilled at identifying investment opportunities. I am normal, and that means I need a lot of training and improvement to become a competitive investor.

Over the last two decades of my career as an investor, I had the help of many great mentors and experienced investors who taught me valuable lessons in investing. I also had a passion for investing that made me stick to the profession – even through prolonged periods of miserable performance and a lot of criticism from my clients (not to mention the dreadful decline in my lifetime savings).

In a way, this book, with its tools to avoid common mistakes, is my way of helping the next generation of investors to learn and improve at a quicker pace than I did. So, as you finish the book, I hope you will consider this not an end, but a beginning. The beginning of a fun ride in financial markets with the goal of becoming a better investor. Over to you and enjoy the ride!